Žižek's Jokes

The MIT Press
Cambridge, Massachusetts
London, England

Žižek's Jokes

(Did you hear the one
about Hegel and negation?)

SLAVOJ ŽIŽEK

EDITED BY AUDUN MORTENSEN
AFTERWORD BY MOMUS

This edition is based upon an earlier publication, *The Collected Jokes of Slavoj Žižek*, published by Flamme Forlag, © 2012 Audun Mortensen.

MIT Press books may be purchased at special quantity discounts for business or sales promotional use. For information, please email special_sales@mitpress.mit.edu.

This book was set in Bembo by the MIT Press. Printed and bound in the United States of America. The image on page 135 was created by Sean Reilly.

Library of Congress Cataloging-in-Publication Data

Žižek, Slavoj.

Žižek's jokes : (did you hear the one about Hegel and negation?) / by Slavoj Žižek ; edited by Audun Mortensen ; afterword by Momus.

p. cm.

Includes bibliographical references.

ISBN 978-0-262-02671-0 (hardcover : alk. paper) 1. Wit and humor—Philosophy. 2. Wit and humor—Psychological aspects. 3. Philosophy—Humor. 4. Joking—Psychological aspects. I. Mortensen, Audun. II. Title.

PN6149.P5Z59 2013

808.87—dc23

2013019607

10 9 8 7 6 5 4 3

CONTENTS

One of the popular myths of the late Communist regimes in Eastern Europe was that there was a department of the secret police whose function was (not to collect, but) to invent and put in circulation political jokes against the regime and its representatives, as they were aware of jokes' positive stabilizing function (political jokes offer to ordinary people an easy and tolerable way to blow off steam, easing their frustrations). Attractive as it is, this myth ignores a rarely mentioned but nonetheless crucial feature of jokes: they never seem to have an author, as if the question "who is the author of this joke?" were an impossible one. Jokes are originally "told," they are always-already "heard" (recall the proverbial "Did you hear that joke about …?"). Therein resides their mystery: they are idiosyncratic, they stand for the unique creativity of language, but are nonetheless "collective," anonymous, authorless, all of a sudden here out of nowhere. The idea that there has to be an author of a joke is properly paranoiac: it means that there has to be an "Other of the Other," of the anonymous symbolic order, as if the very unfathomable contingent generative power of language has to be personalized, located into an agent who controls it and secretly pulls the strings. This is why, from the theological perspective, God is the ultimate jokester. This is the thesis of Isaac Asimov's charming short story "Jokester," about a group of historians of language who, in order to support the hypothesis that God created man out of apes by telling them a joke (he told apes who, up to that moment, were merely exchanging animal signs, the first joke that gave birth to spirit), try to reconstruct this joke, the "mother of all jokes." (Incidentally, for a member of the Judeo-Christian tradition, this work is superfluous, since we all know what this joke was: "Do not eat from the tree of knowledge!"—the first prohibition that clearly is a joke, a perplexing temptation whose point is not clear.)[1]

NOTE

1. *Less Than Nothing* (London: Verso, 2012), 94–95.

ŽIŽEK'S JOKES

THREE WHITES AND TWO BLACKS

We should reread Lacan's text on logical time, where he provides a brilliant interpretation of the logical puzzle of three prisoners. What is not so well known is that the original form of this puzzle comes from the eighteenth-century French libertinage with its mixture of sex and cold logic (which culminates in Sade). In this sexualized version, the governor of a woman's prison has decided that he will give amnesty to one of the three prisoners; the winner will be decided by a test of her intelligence. The three women will be placed in a triangle around a large round table, each naked from the waist below and leaning forward on the table to enable penetration *a tergo*. Each woman will then be penetrated from behind by either a black or a white man, so she will be only able to see the color of the men who are penetrating the other two woman in front of her; all that she will know is that there are only five men available to the governor for this experiment, three white and two black. Given these constraints, the winner will be the woman who first can establish the color of skin of the man fucking her, pushing him away and leaving the room. There are three possible cases here, of increasing complexity:

- In the first case, there are two black men and one white man fucking the women. Since the woman fucked by a white man knows that there are only two black men in the pool, she can immediately rise and leave the room.

- In the second case, there is one black man and two white men doing the fucking. The two women fucked by white men can hence see one white man and one black man. The woman fucked by a black man can see two white men, but—since there are three white men in the pool—she also cannot immediately rise. The only way for a winner to emerge in this second case is if one of the two women being fucked by a white man reasons in this way to herself: "I can see one white man and one black man, so the guy fucking me might be white or black. However, if my fucker was black, the woman in front of me fucked by a white man would see two black men and immediately conclude that her fucker was white—she would have stood up and moved immediately. But she hasn't done this, so my fucker must be white."

- In the third case, each of the three women is being fucked by a white man, so that each of them accordingly sees two other white men. Each can accordingly reason in the same mode as the winner in case 2 had, in the following way: "I can see two white men, so the man fucking me can be white or black. But if mine was black, either of the two others could reason (as the winner in 2 does): 'I can see a black man and a white man. So if my fucker is black, the woman fucked by a white man would see two black man and immediately conclude that her fucker was white and leave. But she hasn't done this. So my fucker must be white.' But since neither of the other two has stood up, my fucker must not be black, but white too."

But here logical time enters. If all three women were of equal intelligence and indeed arose at the same time, this would cast each of them into a radical uncertainty about who is fucking them. Why? Each woman could not know whether the other two women have stood up as a result of going through the same reasoning process she has gone through, since she was being fucked by a white man; or whether each had reasoned as the winner in the second type of case had, because she was fucked by a black man. The winner will be the woman who will be the first to interpret this indecision correctly and jump to the conclusion that it indicates how all three were being fucked by white men.

The consolation prize for the other two women will be that at least they will have been fucked to the end, and this fact gains its meaning the moment one takes note of the political overdetermination of this choice of men: among the upper-class ladies in the mid-eighteenth-century France, black men as sexual partners were, of course, socially unacceptable, but coveted as secret lovers because of their alleged higher potency and supposedly extra-large penises. Consequently, to be fucked by a white man means socially acceptable but intimately not-satisfying sex, while to be fucked by a black man means socially inadmissible but much more satisfying sex. However, this choice is more complex than it may appear, since, in sexual activity, *the fantasy gaze observing us is always here*. The message of the logical puzzle thus becomes more ambiguous: the three women are observing each other while having sex, and what they have to establish is not simply "Who is fucking me, a black or a white guy?" but, rather, "What am I for the Other's gaze while I am being fucked?," as if her very identity is established through this gaze.

THE FUNCTION OF REPETITION is best exemplified by an old joke from Socialist times about a Yugoslav politician on a visit to Germany. When his train passes a city, he asks his guide: "What city is this?" The guide replies: "Baden-Baden." The politician snaps back: "I'm not an idiot—you don't have to tell me twice!"

A SNOBBISH IDIOT goes to an expensive restaurant and, when asked by the waiter: *"Hors d'oeuvre?,"* he replies: "No, I am not out of work, I earn enough to be able to afford to eat here!" The waiter then explains he means the appetizer and proposes raw ham: *"Du jambon cru?"* The idiot replies: "No, I don't believe it was ham I had the last time here. But OK, let's have it now—and quickly, please!" The waiter reassures him: *"J'ai hâte de vous servir!"* to which the idiot snaps back: "Why should you hate to serve me? I will give you a good tip!" And so on, till finally the idiot gets the point that his knowledge of French is limited; to repair his reputation and prove that he is a man of culture, he decides, upon his departure late in the evening, to wish the waiter good night not in French—*"Bonne nuit!"*—afraid that something might go wrong again, but in Latin: *"Nota bene!"*

Do most of the dialogues in philosophy not function in a similar way, especially when a philosopher endeavors to criticize another philosopher? Is not Aristotle's critique of Plato a series of *"Nota bene!"* not to mention Marx's critique of Hegel, etc., etc.?

ONE CAN WELL IMAGINE a truly obscene version of the "aristocrats" joke that easily beats all the vulgarity of family members vomiting, shitting, fornicating, and humiliating each other in all possible ways: when asked to perform, they give the manager a short course in Hegelian thought, debating the true meaning of the negativity, of sublation, of absolute knowing, etc., and, when the surprised manager asks them what is the name of the weird show, they enthusiastically reply: "The Aristocrats!" Indeed, to paraphrase Brecht's quote "What is the robbing of a bank compared to the founding of a bank?": what is the disturbing shock of family members shitting into one another's mouth compared to the shock of a proper dialectical reversal? So, perhaps, one should turn the title of the joke around—the family comes to the manager of a night club specialized in hard-core performances, performs its Hegelian dialogue, and, when asked what is the title of their strange performance, enthusiastically exclaims: "The Perverts!"

THERE IS A NICELY VULGAR JOKE about Christ: the night before he was arrested and crucified, his followers started to worry—Christ was still a virgin; wouldn't it be nice to have him experience a little bit of pleasure before he dies? So they asked Mary Magdalene to go to the tent where Christ was resting and seduce him; Mary said she would do it gladly and went in, but five minutes later, she ran out screaming, terrified and furious. The followers asked her what went wrong, and she explained: "I slowly undressed, spread my legs and showed Christ my pussy; he looked at it, said 'What a terrible wound! It should be healed!' and gently put his palm on it."

So beware of people too intent on healing other people's wounds—what if one enjoys one's wound? In exactly the same way, directly healing the wound of colonialism (effectively returning to the precolonial reality) would have been a nightmare: if today's Indians were to find themselves in precolonial reality, they would have undoubtedly uttered the same terrified scream as Mary Magdalene.

THERE IS A NICE JOKE ABOUT JESUS CHRIST: in order to relax after the arduous work of preaching and performing miracles, Jesus decided to take a short break on the shore of the Sea of Galilee. During a game of golf with one of his apostles, there was a difficult shot to be performed; Jesus did it badly and the ball ended up in the water, so he did his usual trick: he walked on the water to the place where the ball was, reached down and picked it up. When Jesus tried the same shot again, the apostle told him that this is a very difficult one—only someone like Tiger Woods can do it; Jesus replied, "What the hell, I am the son of God, I can do what Tiger Woods can do!" and took another strike. The ball again landed in the water, so Jesus again took a walk on the surface of the water to retrieve it. At this point, a group of American tourists walked by and one of them, observing what was going on, turned to the apostle and said: "My god, who is this guy there? Does he think he is Jesus or what?" The apostle replies: "No, the jerk thinks he is Tiger Woods!"

This is how fantasmatic identification works: no one, not even God himself, is directly what he is; everybody needs an external, decentered point of identification.

THERE ARE THREE REASONS we can be sure that Jesus Christ came from a Jewish family: (1) He took over the profession of his father; (2) his mother thought her son was a god; (3) he couldn't imagine his parents had sexual relations.

HOW CAN WE BE SURE that Judas didn't really betray Jesus Christ? Whatever one thinks about the Jews, they know the value of the things they sell, so no Jew would have sold a god for mere 30 silver talents!

IN THE MID-1930S, a debate is raging in the Politburo of the Bolshevik : will there be money in communism or not? The Leftist Trotskytes claim there will be no money since money is only needed in societies with private ownership, while the Rightist partisans of Bukharin claim that of course there will be money in communism since every complex society needs money to regulate the exchange or products. When, finally, Comrade Stalin intervenes, he rejects both the Leftist and the Rightist deviations, claiming that the truth is a higher dialectical synthesis of the opposites. When other Politburo members ask him how this synthesis will look, Stalin calmly answers: "There will be money and there will not be money. Some will have money and others will not have it."

THE CRUCIAL SHIFT in the "negation of negation" is thus an unexpected change of the very terrain—this change undermines the position of the subject, involving him in the action in a new and much more direct way. Here is a nice case of such a change: at a local Communist Party meeting in Moscow, Petrov is delivering an interminable report. When he notices an obviously bored man in the first row, he asks him: "Hey, you, do you know who this Bulianoff I was just talking about is?" "No idea who he is," answers the man, and Petrov snaps back: "You see, if you were to come to the party meetings more often and listen more carefully, you would have known who Bulianoff is!" The man snaps back: "But do you, Petrov, know who Andreyev is?" Petrov replies: "No, I don't know any Andreyev." The man calmly concludes: "If you were to attend the party meeting less often and listen more carefully to what is going on in your home, you would have known that Andreyev is the guy who is fucking your wife while you are delivering your boring speeches!"

A SIMILAR UNEXPECTED TURN toward vulgarity is enacted in the joke from the mid-1990s celebrating Bill Clinton's seductive capacity: Clinton and the pope die on the same day; however, owing to the confusion in the divine administration, Clinton ends up in heaven and the pope in hell. After a couple of days, the mistake is noticed and the two are ordered to exchange places; they briefly meet in front of the elevator that connects heaven and hell. Upon seeing Clinton on his way from heaven, the pope asks him: "Tell me, how is the Virgin Mary? I cannot wait to meet her!" Clinton replies with a smile: "Sorry, but she is no longer a virgin."

THE MEANING OF A SCENE can change entirely with the shift in the subjective point, as in a classic Soviet joke in which Brezhnev dies and is taken to Hell; however, since he was a great leader, he is given the privilege to be taken on a tour and select his room there. The guide opens a door and Brezhnev sees Khruschev sitting on a sofa, passionately kissing and fondling Marilyn Monroe in his lap; he joyously exclaims: "I wouldn't mind being in this room!" The guide snaps back: "Don't be too eager, comrade! This is not the room in hell for Khruschev, but for Marilyn Monroe!"

A JOKE FROM THE EARLY 1960S nicely renders the paradox of the presupposed belief. After Yuri Gagarin, the first cosmonaut, made his visit to space, he was received by Nikita Khruschev, the general secretary of the Communist Party, and told him confidentially: "You know, comrade, that up there in the sky, I saw heaven with God and angels—Christianity is right!" Khruschev whispers back to him: "I know, I know, but keep quiet, don't tell this to anyone!" Next week, Gagarin visited the Vatican and was received by the pope, to whom he confides: "You know, holy father, I was up there in the sky and I saw there is no God or angels …" "I know, I know," interrupts the pope, "but keep quiet, don't tell this to anyone!"

ONE CAN EVEN DEVELOP into a Hegelian triad the lines from Psalm 23:4: "Even though I walk through the valley of the shadow of death, I will fear no evil, for you are with me; your rod and your staff, they comfort me." Its first negation would have been a radical reversal of the subjective position, as in the ghetto-rapper-version: "Even though I walk through the valley of the shadow of death, I will fear no evil, for I am the meanest motherfucker in the whole valley!" Then comes the negation of negation that changes the entire field by way of "deconstructing" the opposition of Good and Evil: "Even though I walk through the valley of the shadow of death, I will fear no evil, for I know that Good and Evil are just metaphysical binary opposites!"

THE LOGIC OF THE HEGELIAN TRIAD can be perfectly rendered by the three versions of the relationship between sex and migraines. We begin with the classic scene: a man wants sex with his wife, and she replies: "Sorry, darling, I have a terrible migraine, I can't do it now!" This starting position is then negated/inverted with the rise of feminist liberation—it is the wife who now demands sex and the poor tired man who replies: "Sorry, darling, I have a terrible migraine ..." In the concluding moment of the negation of negation that again inverts the entire logic, this time making the argument against into an argument for, the wife claims: "Darling, I have a terrible migraine, so let's have some sex to refresh me!" And one can even imagine a rather depressive moment of radical negativity between the second and the third versions: the husband and the wife both have migraines and agree to just have a quiet cup of tea.

AFTER ORPHEUS TURNS AROUND to cast a glance at Euridice and thus loses her, the Divinity consoles him—true, he has lost her as a flesh-and-blood person, but from now on, he will be able to discern her beautiful features everywhere, in the stars in the sky, in the glistening of the morning dew. Orpheus is quick to accept the narcissistic profit of this reversal: he becomes enraptured with the poetic glorification of Euridice that lies ahead of him; to put it succinctly, he no longer loves HER, what he loves is the vision of HIMSELF displaying his love for her.

This, of course, throws a new comic light on the eternal question of why Orpheus looked back and thus screwed things up. What we encounter here is simply the link between the death-drive and creative sublimation: Orpheus's backward gaze is a perverse act *stricto sensu;* he loses Euridice intentionally in order to regain her as the object of sublime poetic inspiration. (This idea was developed by Klaus Theweleit.) But should one not go even a step further? What if Euridice herself, aware of the impasse of her beloved Orpheus, intentionally provoked his turning around? What if her reasoning was something like: "I know he loves me; but he is potentially a great poet, this is his fate, and he cannot fulfill that promise by being happily married to me—so the only ethical thing for me to do is to sacrifice myself, to provoke him into turning around and losing me, so that he will be able to become the great poet he deserves to be"—and then she starts gently coughing or something similar to attract his attention.

TWO JEWISH FRIENDS pass a Catholic church on which a large poster addresses non-Catholics: "Come to us, accept Catholicism, and you instantly get $30,000 in cash!" While walking away, the two friends become engaged in a debate about whether the offer is meant seriously. A week later, the two friends meet again in front of the same church, and one of them confides to the other: "I still wonder if that offer is serious." The other replies condescendingly: "Ah you Jews, all you think about is money!"

WHEN THE TURKISH COMMUNIST WRITER Panait Istrati visited the Soviet Union in the mid-1930s, the time of the big purges and show trials, a Soviet apologist trying to convince him about the need for violence against the enemies evoked the proverb "You can't make an omelet without breaking eggs," to which Istrati tersely replied: "All right. I can see the broken eggs. Where's this omelet of yours?"

We should say the same about the austerity measures imposed by IMF: the Greeks would have the full right to say, "OK, we are breaking our eggs for all of Europe, but where's the omelet you are promising us?"

IN ONE OF THE ANTI-SOVIET JOKES popular after the Soviet invasion of Czechoslovakia in 1968, a fairy queen approaches a Czech and tells him that she is ready to grant him three wishes; the Czech immediately puts forward the first wish: "The Chinese army should occupy my country for a month and then withdraw!" After the fairy queen asks him for the other two wishes, he says: "The same once more! The Chinese should occupy us again and again!" When the bewildered queen asks him why he chose this weird wish, the Czech answers with a malicious grin: "Because each time the Chinese would occupy us, they would have to pass through the Soviet Union on their way here and back!"

The same often holds for "feminine masochism," and especially for du Maurier stories with their heroines enjoying their painful passions: they follow the logic of displacement; that is, to interpret them properly, one should focus the attention on the third (male) subject who is targeted when a woman is repeatedly "occupied by the Chinese army."

THERE ARE GOOD REASONS to accept that the Christian topic of immaculate conception is grounded in the mistranslation of the Hebrew *alma* (which simply means "young woman") as "virgin": "It would appear that Western civilization has endured two millennia of consecrated sexual neurosis simply because the authors of Matthew and Luke could not read Hebrew" (Harris, *The End of Faith*). There are also good reasons to accept that the seventy "virgins" awaiting martyrs in the Muslim paradise resulted from a mistranslation: in using the word *hur*, transliterated as "houris," the Koran relied here on the early Christian texts that used the Aramaic *hur*, meaning "white raisins," a delicacy. Let us take a young martyr on a suicide mission because he took literally his leader's promise: "The gates of Paradise have opened for you. There are beautiful black-eyed virgins waiting for you on the banks of rivers of honey." Imagine the look on his face "when, finding himself in a paradise teeming with his fellow thugs, his seventy houris arrive as a fistful of raisins."

In a classic Bosnian joke, a guy visits his best friend and finds him playing tennis in a backyard court—Agassi, Sampras, and other world-class players are there waiting for a game with him. Surprised, the guy asks his friend: "But you were never much of a tennis player! How did you manage to improve your game so fast?" The friend answers: "You see that pond behind my house? There is a magic golden fish in it; if you tell her a wish, she immediately realizes it!" The friend goes to the pond, sees the fish, tells her that he wants his closet full of money, and runs home to check on it. When he approaches his closet, he sees honey dripping out from it everywhere. Furious, he runs back to his friend and tells him: "But I wanted money, not honey!" The friend calmly replies: "Oh, I forgot to tell you—the fish has impaired hearing and sometimes misunderstands the wish. Can't you see how bored I am running around and playing this stupid game? Do you think that I really asked for an outstanding tennis game?" Is there not a Kafkaesque twist to this story, exactly homologous to that of the poor Muslim warrior being offered a fistful of raisins?

THERE IS A NICELY VULGAR contemporary Bosnian joke about Beethoven's popular piano piece "Für Elise" ("For Elisa"), making fun of the "enlightened" West European teachers sent to civilize "primitive" Bosnians. In a high school class on music history, a female teacher says that they will not deal with Beethoven in a traditional way, learning the facts, but more creatively: every pupil will mention an idea or image and then name a Beethoven piece that fits it. First, a shy girl says: "A beautiful green meadow in front of a forest, with a deer drinking water from a stream … Pastoral Symphony!" A boy follows her: "Revolutionary war, heroism, freedom … Eroica!" Finally, a Bosnian boy says: "A big, thick, strong, erect cock." "What is this for?," asks the annoyed teacher. "For Elisa!"

The boy's remark obeys the logic of the phallic signifier "suturing" the series, not because it explicitly mentions the organ, but because it concludes the series by way of shift from metaphor to metonymy: while the first two pupils were providing metaphoric meaning (the Pastoral Symphony signifies/evokes a meadow with a stream, etc.), the erect cock mentioned by the Bosnian boy doesn't mean or evoke Elisa, it is to be used by her to satisfy her sexually. (The additional obscene implication, of course, is that the teacher herself is sexually starved, in need of a good lay that will stop her bothering her pupils with such stupid tasks.)

A TOUCH OF COMIC REVERSAL pertains to Café Photo in São Paolo: publicized as "entertainment with a special touch," it is—so I was told—a meeting place for high-class prostitutes with their prospective clients. Although this fact is very well known by the public, the information is not officially published on their website—the official statement is that "it is a place to meet the best company for your evening." Things really proceed there with a special touch: prostitutes themselves—mostly students of humanities—choose their customers. Men (prospective clients) enter, take a seat at a table, buy a drink, and wait, while being observed by women. If a woman finds one of them acceptable, she seats herself at his table, lets him buy her a drink, and starts a conversation on some intellectual topic, usually a theme on cultural life, sometimes even art theory. If she finds the man bright and attractive enough, she asks him if he would like to go to bed with her and tells him her price. This is prostitution with a feminist twist, if there ever was one—however, as is often the case, the feminist twist is paid for by a class limitation: both prostitutes and clients come from the upper or at least upper-middle class.

A COUPLE OF YEARS AGO, Slovene feminists reacted with a great outcry to the publicity poster of a large cosmetics factory that made suntan lotion, depicting a series of well-tanned women's behinds in tight bathing suits, accompanied with the logo "Each has her own factor." Of course, this publicity is based on a rather vulgar double-entendre: the logo ostensibly refers to the suntan lotion, which is offered to customers with different sun-protection factors for different skin types; however, its entire effect is based on its obvious male-chauvinist reading: "Each woman can be had, if only the man knows her factor, her specific catalyst, what arouses her!" The Freudian point regarding fundamental fantasy would be that each subject, female or male, possesses such a "factor" that regulates her or his desire: "a woman, viewed from behind, on her hands and knees" was the Wolfman's factor; a statue—like a woman without pubic hair—was Ruskin's factor; etc., etc. There is nothing uplifting about our awareness of this "factor": this awareness can never be subjectivized; it is uncanny, even horrifying, since it somehow "depossesses" the subject, reducing her or him to a puppet-like level "beyond dignity and freedom."

THE DEBATE ABOUT WHETHER or not waterboarding is torture should be dropped as obvious nonsense: how, if not by causing pain and fear of death, does waterboarding make hardened terrorist-suspects talk? As to the replacement of the word "torture" with "enhanced interrogation technique," one should note that we are dealing here with an extension of Politically Correct logic: in exactly the same way that "disabled" becomes "physically challenged," "torture" becomes "enhanced interrogation technique" (and, why not, "rape" could become "enhanced seduction technique"). The crucial point is that torture—brutal violence practiced by the state—was made publicly acceptable at the very moment when public language was rendered Politically Correct in order to protect victims from symbolic violence. These two phenomena are the two sides of the same coin.

THERE IS A UNIQUE COMICAL MOMENT in Kierkegaard's *Concept of Anxiety* where he describes in a mockingly anti-Hegelian way how Simon Tornacensis (the thirteenth-century Parisian scholastic theologian) "thought that God must be obliged to him for having furnished a proof of the Trinity. ... This story has numerous analogies, and in our time speculation has assumed such authority that it has practically tried to make God feel uncertain of himself, like a monarch who is anxiously waiting to learn whether the general assembly will make him an absolute or a limited monarch."

Kierkegaard of course dismisses the attempts to logically demonstrate the existence of God as absurd and pointless logical exercises (his model of such professorial blindness for the authentic religious experience was Hegel's dialectical machinery); however, his sense of humor cannot withstand the wonderful image of God in anxiety, dreading for his own status as if it depends on the logical exercises of a philosopher, as if the philosopher's reasoning has consequences in the real, so that, if the proof fails, God's existence itself is threatened. And one can go even further in this line of Kierkegaardian reasoning: what undoubtedly attracted him to the remark of Tornacensis was the blasphemous idea of a God himself in anxiety. The political parallel here is crucial, since Kierkegaard himself resorts to the comparison of God and king: God exposed to the philosopher's whimsy is like a king exposed to the whimsy of a popular assembly.

But what is his point here? Is it simply that, in both cases, we should reject liberal decadence and opt for absolute monarchy? What complicates this simple and apparently obvious solution is that, for Kierkegaard, the (properly comical) point of the Incarnation is that that God-king becomes a beggar, a low ordinary human. Would it thus not be more correct to conceive Christianity as the paradox of God's abdication—God steps down to be replaced by the assembly of believers called the Holy Spirit?

THERE ARE MANY OBJECTS or gadgets that promise to deliver excessive pleasure but that effectively reproduce only its absence. The latest fashion is the Stamina Training Unit, a counterpart to the vibrator: a masturbatory device that resembles a battery-powered light (so we're not embarrassed when carrying it around). You put your erect penis into the opening at the top, push the button, and the object vibrates until satisfaction. The product is available in different colors, sizes, and forms (hairy or hairless, etc.) that imitate all three main openings for sexual penetration (mouth, vagina, anus). What one buys here is the partial object (erogenous zone) alone, deprived of the embarrassing additional burden of the entire person. How are we to cope with this brave new world that undermines the basic premises of our intimate life? The ultimate solution would be, of course, to push a vibrator into the Stamina Training Unit, turn them both on and leave all the fun to this ideal couple, with us, the two real human partners, sitting at a nearby table, drinking tea and calmly enjoying the fact that, without great effort, we have fulfilled our duty to enjoy. So maybe, if our hands meet while pouring tea, we may end up in bed as part of a real romance, enjoying it outside any superego pressure to enjoy.

IN AN OLD YUGOSLAV JOKE mocking police corruption, a policeman returns home unexpectedly and finds his wife naked in their marital bed, obviously hot and excited. Suspecting that he surprised her with a lover, he starts to look around the room for a hidden man. The wife goes pale when he leans down to look under the bed; but after some brief whispering, the husband rises with a satisfied, smug smile and says "Sorry, my love, false alarm. There is no one under the bed!," while his hand is holding tightly a couple of high denomination banknotes.

WHEN THE UNCONDITIONAL CHRISTIAN fundamen-
talist supporters of Israeli politics reject leftist critiques
of Israeli policies, their implicit line of argumentation is
best rendered by a wonderful cartoon published in July
2008 in the Viennese daily *Die Presse*: it shows two stocky
Nazi-looking Austrians, one of them holding in his hands
a newspaper and commenting to his friend: "Here you
can see again how totally justified anti-Semitism is being
misused for a cheap critique of Israel!" THESE are today's
allies of the state of Israel.[1]

YEARS AGO, ON THE CAMPUS OF SANTA CRUZ, one of the capitals of Political Correctness, I was told that that they developed jokes that are funny without hurting, humiliating, or even making fun of anyone, like "what happens when a triangle meets a circle?" As one might expect, I immediately exploded back: I don't care what happens when a triangle meets a circle; the whole enjoyment of a joke is that there must be someone who is hurt, humiliated ... But what if was I wrong, what if I missed the purely formal aspect that is what makes a joke funny much more than its direct content, in the same way that sexuality is not a matter of direct content, but of the way this content is formally treated? The question is, of course, can this form do its work alone, or does it need "a little piece of reality" in the sense of some contingent positive content related to "dirty" topics (sex, violence)?[2]

IN A WONDERFULLY STUPID (and apolitical!) Russian joke from the time of the Soviet Union, two strangers sit in the same train compartment. After a long silence, one suddenly addresses the other: "Have you ever fucked a dog?" Surprised, the other replies: "No—have you?" "Of course not. That's disgusting. I just asked it to start a conversation!"[3]

IN CHINA, THE LOCAL PARTY BOSSES are popular targets of obscene jokes that mock their vulgar tastes and sexual obsessions. (Far from emanating from ordinary people, these jokes mostly express the attitude of the higher *nomenklatura* toward the lower cadres.) In one of them, a small provincial party boss has just returned from the big city where he bought himself expensive shiny new black shoes. When his young secretary brings him tea, he wants to impress her with the quality of his shoes; so when she leans over his table and his foot is under her, he tells her that he can see (reflected in his shoe) that her underpants are blue; the next day the flirting goes on, and he tells her that today her underpants are green. On the third day, the secretary decides to come without underpants; looking at his shoes for the reflection, the party boss desperately exclaims: "I've just bought these shoes, and already there's a large crack on their surface!"

In the final displacement, precisely when the boss is able to see the reflected "thing itself" (the vaginal crack, no longer just the underpants covering it), he withdraws from recognizing it and reads it as the feature of the mirror reflecting it (the crack of his polished shoes). One can even detect here, beneath the surface of the boss's vulgar boastfulness, a sign of hidden politeness: in a gentle misrecognition, he prefers to appear as an idiot rather than to declare rudely what he can see. The procedure here is different from that of fetishist displacement: the subject's perception doesn't stop at the last thing he sees before the direct view of the vaginal opening (as in the fetishist fixation); that is, his shoe is not his fetish, the last thing he sees before seeing the vaginal crack; when, unexpectedly and inadvertently, he does get a view of the vaginal crack, he assumes the crack as his own, as his own deficiency.[4]

A JOKE THAT RENDERS THE HEGELIAN TRIAD inclusive of the final "reconciliation" is a particularly cruel variation of the first-bad-news–then-good-news medical jokes, encompassing the entire triad of good-bad-good news. After his wife had undergone a long and risky operation, the husband approaches the doctor and inquires about the outcome. The doctor begins: "Your wife survived; she will probably live longer than you. But there are some complications: she will no longer be able to control her anal muscles, so shit will drift continuously out of her anus. There will also be a continuous flow of a bad smelling yellow jelly from her vagina, so any sex is out. Plus her mouth will malfunction and food will be falling out of it." Noting the growing expression of panic on the husband's face, the doctor taps him friendly on the shoulder and smiles: "Don't worry, I was just joking! Everything is OK—she died during the operation."[5]

THERE IS A WONDERFULLY VULGAR JEWISH JOKE about a Polish-Jewish wife, tired after a hard day's work; when her husband comes home, also tired, but horny, he tells her: "I cannot make love to you now, but I need a release—can you suck me and swallow my sperm? That would help me a lot!" The wife replies: "I am too tired to do that now, darling—why don't you just masturbate into a glass, and I will drink it in the morning!"

Does this wife—contrary to the cliché about the holistic-intuitive reasoning of women as opposed to the masculine rational analysis—not provide an example of the ruthless feminine use of Understanding, of its power to separate what naturally belongs together?[6]

RECALL THE ITALIAN EXPRESSION *se non è vero, è ben trovato*—"even if it is not true, it is well conceived." In this sense, anecdotes about famous persons, even when invented, often characterize the core of their personality more appropriately than the enumeration of their real qualities— here also, "truth has the structure of a fiction," as Lacan put it. There is a wonderfully obscene Serbo-Croat version of this expression that perfectly renders the protopsychotic rejection of the symbolic fiction: *se non è vero, jebem ti mater!* "Jebem ti mater" (pronounced "yebem ti mater," meaning "I'll fuck your mother") is one of the most popular vulgar insults; the joke, of course, relies on the perfect correspondence, with the same accents and number of syllables, between *e ben trovato* and *jebem ti mater*. The meaning thus changes into the explosion of rage in the incestuous direction, attacking the other's most intimate primordial object: "It better be true—if it is not true, I'll fuck your mother!" These two versions thus clearly enact the two reactions to what literally turns out to be a lie: its furious rejection, or its "subl(im)ation" into a "higher" truth. In psychoanalytic terms, their difference is the one between foreclosure (*Verwerfung*) and symbolic transubstantiation.[7]

WE ALL KNOW THE OLD JOKE referring to the enigma of who really wrote Shakespeare's plays: "Not William Shakespeare, but someone else with the same name." This is what Lacan means by the "decentered subject"; this is how a subject relates to the name that fixes its symbolic identity: John Smith is (always, by definition, in its very notion) not John Smith, but someone else with the same name. As Shakespeare's Juliet knew, I am never "that name"—the John Smith who really thinks he is John Smith is a psychotic.[8]

THIS LACK OR IMPERFECTION of the (big) Other is rendered in a wonderfully simple way in a joke about two friends who are playing a game where you have to hit a can with a ball. After repeated kicks, one of them says: "For the devil's sake, I missed it!" His friend, a religious fanatic, comments: "How dare you talk like that; it's blasphemy! May God strike you with lightning as punishment!" A moment later, lightning does strike, but it hits the religious guy who, shaken and barely alive, turns his gaze up and asks: "But why did you hit me, my Lord, and not the culprit?" A deep voice resonates from above: "For the devil's sake, I missed!"[9]

SUCH AN IMPOSSIBLE POINT OF VIEW is often mobilized in jokes. A contemporary Chinese sexual joke reports on a conversation between twin brothers who are still fetuses in their mother's womb; one says to the other: "I love it when our father visits us, but why is he so rude at the end of each visit, spitting all over us?" The other replies: "True, our uncle is much nicer: he always comes with a nice hat made of rubber on his head, so that he doesn't spit on us!"[10]

IN AN OLD SLOVENE JOKE, a young schoolboy has to write a short composition with a title "There is only one mother!," in which he is expected to illustrate, apropos a singular experience, the love that links him to his mother; here is what he writes: "One day I returned home earlier than expected, because the teacher was ill; I looked for my mother and found her naked in her bed with a man who was not my father. My mother angrily shouted at me: "What are you staring at like an idiot? Why don't you run to the refrigerator and get us two cold beers!" I ran to the kitchen, opened the refrigerator, looked into it, and shouted back to the bedroom: "There is only one, mother!"

Is this not a supreme case of interpretation that just adds a punctuation mark that changes everything, as in the parody of the first words of *Moby-Dick*: "Call me, Ishmael!"? One can discern the same operation in Heidegger (the way he reads "Nothing is without reason (*nihil est sine ratione*)," by shifting the accent to "Nothing[ness] IS without reason"), or in the superego displacement of the prohibitive injunction of the symbolic law (from "Don't kill!" to "Don't!" … "Kill!"). However, one should risk a more detailed interpretation. The joke stages a Hamlet-like confrontation of the son with the enigma of mother's excessive desire; in order to escape this deadlock, the mother as it were takes refuge in /the desire for/ an external partial object, the bottle of beer, destined to divert the son's attention from the obscene Thing of her being caught naked in bed with a man—the message of this demand is: "You see, even if I am in bed with a man, my desire is for something else that you can bring me. I am not excluding you by getting completely caught in the circle of passion with this man!" The two bottles of beer / also/ stand for the elementary signifying dyad, like Lacan's famous two restroom doors observed by two children from the train window in his "Instance of the letter in the unconscious"; from this perspective, the child's repartee is to be read as rendering to the mother the elementary Lacanian lesson: "Sorry, mother, but there is ONLY ONE SIGNIFIER, for the man only, there is no binary signifier (for the woman), this signifier is *ur-verdraengt*, primordially repressed!" In short: you are caught naked, you are not covered by the signifier. And what of this is the fundamental message of monotheism? Not the reduction of the Other to the One, but, on the contrary, the acceptance of the fact that the binary signifier always-already lacks. This imbalance between the One and its "primordially repressed" counterpart is the radical difference, in contrast to the big cosmological couples (*yin* and *yang*, etc.) that can emerge only within the horizon of the undifferentiated One (*tao*, etc.). And are not even the attempts to introduce a balanced duality into the minor spheres of consummation, like the couple of small blue and red bags of artificial sweetener available everywhere in cafés, yet another desperate attempt to provide a symmetrical signifying couple for the sexual difference (blue "masculine" bags versus red "feminine" bags)? The point is not that sexual difference is the ultimate signified of all such couples, but rather that the proliferation of such couples displays an attempt to supplement the LACK of the founding binary signifying couple that would directly stand for sexual difference.[11]

TO GRASP MORE CLOSELY this non-All, let us turn to a wonderful dialectical joke in Lubitsch's *Ninotchka*: the hero visits a cafeteria and orders coffee without cream; the waiter replies: "Sorry, but we have run out of cream. Can I bring you coffee without milk?" In both cases, the customer gets coffee alone, but this One-coffee is each time accompanied by a different negation, first coffee-with-no-cream, then coffee-with-no-milk. (In a similar way, Eastern Europeans in 1990 did not only want democracy-without-communism, but also democracy-without-capitalism.) What we encounter here is the logic of differentiality, where the lack itself functions as a positive feature—the paradox rendered nicely by an old Yugoslav joke about a Montenegrin (people from Montenegro were stigmatized as lazy in the former Yugoslavia): why does a Montenegro guy, when going to sleep, put at the side of his bed two glasses, one full and one empty? Because he is too lazy to think in advance if he will be thirsty during the night. The point of this joke is that the absence itself has to be positively registered: it is not enough to have one full glass of water, since, if the Montenegrin will not be thirsty, he will simply ignore it—this negative fact itself has to be taken note of by the empty glass, that is, no-need-for water has to be materialized in the void of the empty glass. There is a political equivalent of these lines: in a joke from Socialist Poland, a customer enters a store and asks: "You probably don't have butter, or do you?" The answer: "Sorry, but we are the store that doesn't have toilet paper; the one across the street is the one that doesn't have butter!"[12]

SIMILAR (BUT NOT THE SAME) is the legendary answer of a Hearst newspaper editor to Hearst's inquiry why he doesn't want to take a long-deserved holiday: "I am afraid that if I go, there will be chaos; everything will fall apart—but I am even more afraid to discover that, if I go, things will just go on as normal without me, a proof that I am not really needed!" A certain negative choice (no holiday, seeing a film again) is supported both by yes and no; however, what one should be attentive to is the asymmetry of the answers, and this asymmetry resorts clearly if we imagine the dialogue as a succession of two answers: first, the reaction is the obvious (negative) one (I didn't like the film; I am afraid everything will fall apart if I take a holiday); then, when this reaction fails to produce the desired goal, the opposite (positive) reason is given (I liked the film; everything will be OK without me), which fails even more miserably. No wonder that one can reformulate the Hearst editor's double answer as a dialogue along the lines of the Rabinovitch joke: "Why don't you take a holiday, you deserved it!" "I don't want to go, for two reasons. First, I am afraid that everything will fall apart here if I take a holiday." "But you are totally wrong; you will see that things will just go on as normal when you're not here!" "That is my second reason."[13]

AND HOW CAN WE NOT MENTION here another incident involving coffee from the popular cinema, this time from the English working-class drama *Brassed Off*? The hero accompanies home a pretty young woman who, at the entrance to her flat, tells him: "Would you like to come in for a coffee?" To his answer—"There is a problem—I don't drink coffee"—she retorts with a smile: "No problem—I don't have any." The immense direct erotic power of her reply resides in how—through a double negation, again—she pronounces an embarrassingly direct sexual invitation without ever mentioning sex: when she first invites the guy in for a coffee and then admits she has no coffee, she does not cancel her invitation, she just makes it clear that the first invitation for a coffee was a stand-in (or pretext), indifferent in itself, for the invitation to sex. Along the same lines, one can imagine a dialogue between the United States and Europe in late 2002, when the invasion of Iraq was being prepared: the United States says to Europe: "Would you care to join us in the attack on Iraq to find the WMD!"; Europe replies: "But we have no facilities to search for the WMD!"; Rumsfeld answers: "No problem; there are no WMD in Iraq."[14]

THERE IS A JOKE ABOUT COOKING that relies on the same logic: "Here is how anyone can make a good soup in one hour: prepare all the ingredients, cut the vegetables, etc., boil the water, put the ingredients into it, cook them at a simmer for half an hour, stirring occasionally; when, after three quarters of an hour, you discover that the soup is tasteless and unpalatable, throw it away, open up a good can of soup, and quickly warm it up in a microwave oven. This is how we humans make soup."[15]

THE GOD THAT WE GET HERE is rather like the one from the old Bolshevik joke about an able Communist propagandist who, after his death, finds himself in hell, where he quickly convinces the guards to let him leave and go to heaven instead. When the Devil notices his absence, he quickly pays a visit to God, demanding that he return to hell what belongs to the Devil. However, immediately after the Devil starts to address God: "My Lord ..." God interrupts him: "First, I am not Lord but a comrade. Second, are you crazy talking to a fictional being?—I don't exist! And third, be short, otherwise I'll miss my party cell meeting!"

This is the God today's radical Left needs: a God who wholly "became man"—a comrade among us, crucified together with two social outcasts—and who not only "doesn't exist" but also *himself knows this*, accepting his erasure, entirely passing over into the love that binds members of the Holy Ghost (the party, the emancipatory collective).[16]

THERE IS AN OLD JEWISH JOKE, loved by Derrida, about a group of Jews in a synagogue publicly admitting their nullity in the eyes of God. First, a rabbi stands up and says: "O God, I know I am worthless. I am nothing!" After he has finished, a rich businessman stands up and says, beating himself on the chest: "O God, I am also worthless, obsessed with material wealth. I am nothing!" After this spectacle, a poor ordinary Jew also stands up and also proclaims: "O God, I am nothing." The rich businessman kicks the rabbi and whispers in his ear with scorn: "What insolence! Who is that guy who dares to claim that he is nothing too!"[17]

ULTIMATELY, THERE ARE ONLY TWO OPTIONS, two ways to account for the "magical trick" of the Hegelian synthesis, and they are structured like the two versions of the vulgar doctor's joke of "first-the-bad-news-then-the-good-news." The first one is that the good news is the bad news, just viewed from a different perspective ("The bad news is that we've discovered you have severe Alzheimer's disease. The good news is the same: you have Alzheimer's, so you will have forgotten the bad news by the time you get back home.") There is, however, another version: the good news is good, but it concerns *another* subject ("The bad news is that you have terminal cancer and will die in a month. The good news is: you see that young, beautiful nurse over there? I've been trying to get her into bed for months; finally, yesterday, she said yes and we made love the whole night like crazy."). The true Hegelian "synthesis" is the synthesis of these two options: the good news is the bad news itself—but in order for us to see that, we have to shift to a different agent (from the bird that dies to another one that replaces it; from the cancer-ridden patient to the happy doctor; from Christ as individual to the community of believers).[18]

VARIATIONS

- What if the logic of the old medical joke about Alzheimer's ("The bad news is we've discovered you have severe Alzheimer's disease. The good news is you will have already forgotten the bad news by the time you get home") also applies here, in the case of the post-traumatic loss of personality, so that, when the patient's old personality is destroyed, the very measure of his suffering also disappears?[19]

- There is the ultimate good news/bad news doctor joke that reaches the dark limit of a joke; it starts with the good news, which, however, is so ominous that no further bad news is needed: "Doctor: First the good news: we definitely established that you are not a hypochondriac." No need for a counterpoint here. (Another version: "Doctor: I have some good news and some bad news. Patient: What's the good news? Doctor: The good news is that your name will be soon a household name all around the world—they are naming a disease after you!") Is this a nondialectical short circuit? Or is it rather the proper dialectical beginning that immediately negates itself? Something like this joke happens at the beginning of Hegel's logic, not a passage to the opposite, but the beginning's immediate self-sabotage.

THERE IS AN OLD JOKE ABOUT A HUSBAND who returns home earlier than usual from work and finds his wife in bed with another man. The surprised wife exclaims: "Why have you come back early?" The husband furiously snaps back: "What are you doing in bed with another man?" The wife calmly replies: "I asked you first—don't try to wiggle out of it by changing the subject!"[20]

"POPULISM" IS THUS by definition a negative phenomenon, a phenomenon grounded in a refusal, even an implicit admission of impotence. We all know the old joke about a guy looking for his lost key under the street light; when asked where he lost it, he admits that it was in a dark corner. So why is he looking for it here, under the light? Because the visibility is much better here. There is always something of this trick in populism. It looks for the causes of troubles in the Jews, since they are more visible than complex social processes.[21]

THE REASON I FIND BADIOU PROBLEMATIC is that, for me, something is wrong with the very notion that one can excessively "enforce" a truth: one is almost tempted to apply the logic of the joke quoted by Lacan: "My fiancée is never late for an appointment, because the moment she is late, she is no longer my fiancée." A Truth is never enforced, because the moment fidelity to Truth functions as an excessive enforcement, we are no longer dealing with a Truth, with fidelity to a Truth-Event.[22]

VARIATIONS

- It is a little bit like the proverbial joke "My fiancée is never late for an appointment, because if she is late, she is no longer my fiancée": if you love God, you can do whatever you like, because when you do something evil, this is in itself proof that you do not really love God.[23]

- There is a story (apocryphal, maybe) about the Left-Keynesian economist John Galbraith: before a trip to the USSR in the late 1950s, he wrote to his anti-Communist friend Sidney Hook: "Don't worry, I will not be seduced by the Soviets and return home claiming they have Socialism!" Hook answered him promptly: "But that's what worries me—that you will return claiming the USSR is NOT socialist!" What worried Hook was the naive defense of the purity of the concept: if things go wrong with building a Socialist society, this does not invalidate the idea itself; it just means we didn't implement it properly. Do we not detect the same naivete in today's market fundamentalists? When, during a recent TV debate in France, Guy Sorman claimed that democracy and capitalism necessarily go together, I couldn't resist asking him the obvious question: "But what about China today?" He snapped back: "In China there is no capitalism!" For a fanatically procapitalist Sorman, if a country is nondemocratic, it simply means it is not truly capitalist but practices its disfigured version, in exactly the same way that for a democratic communist Stalinism was simply not an authentic form of communism.

The underlying mistake is not difficult to identify—it is the same as in the joke: "My fiancée is never late for an appointment, because the moment she is late she is no longer my fiancée!" This is how today's apologist of the market, in an unheard-of ideological kidnapping, explains the crisis of 2008: it was not the failure of the free market which caused it but the excessive state regulation, that is, the fact that our market economy was not a true one, that it was still in the clutches of the welfare-state.

- What we have here is a somewhat crueler version of the joke: "My fiancée never misses an appointment with me because the moment she misses one, she is no longer my fiancée"—the people always support the party because any member of the people who opposes party rule automatically excludes himself from the people.[24]

- Let us, in passing, be attentive to the homology between this "skeptical paradox" and the structure of a joke Lacan often refers to: "My fiancée never misses an appointment with me, since the moment she misses it, she is no longer my fiancée."—"I never make a mistake in applying a rule, since what I do defines the very rule."[25]

ALTHOUGH "REALLY EXISTING SOCIALISM" has already receded into a distance that confers upon it the nostalgic magic of a postmodern lost object, some of us still recall a well-known Polish anticommunist joke from the epoch of "really existing socialism": "Socialism is the synthesis of the greatest achievements of all previous modes of production: from preclass tribal society it takes primitivism, from the Asiatic mode of production it takes despotism, from antiquity it takes slavery, from feudalism it takes the social domination of lords over serfs, from capitalism it takes exploitation, and from socialism it takes the name." Does the anti-Semitic figure of the Jew not obey exactly the same logic? It takes from great capitalists their wealth and social control, from the hedonists sexual debauchery, from commercialized popular culture and the yellow press their vulgarity, from the lower classes their filth and bad smell, from intellectuals their corrupted sophistry, *and from Jews their name.*[26]

IT IS NOT THAT THIS CALL for more passion in politics is in itself meaningless (of course the contemporary Left needs more passion); the problem is rather that it resembles all too much the joke quoted by Lacan about a doctor asked by a friend for free medical advice: unwilling to give his services without payment, the doctor examines the friend and then calmly states: "You need medical advice!"[27]

A COUPLE OF YEARS AGO, a charming publicity spot for a beer was shown on British TV. Its first part staged the well-known fairy tale: a girl walks along a stream, sees a frog, takes it gently into her lap, and kisses it; of course, the ugly frog miraculously turns into a beautiful young man. However, the story wasn't finished: the young man casts a covetous glance at the girl, draws her toward himself, and kisses her—and she turns into a bottle of beer, which the man holds triumphantly in his hand. For the woman, the point is that her love and affection (signaled by the kiss) turn a frog into a beautiful man, a full phallic presence; for the man, it is to reduce the woman to a partial object, the cause of his desire (the *objet petit a*). On account of this asymmetry, there is no sexual relationship: we have either a woman with a frog or a man with a bottle of beer. What we can never obtain is the natural couple of a beautiful woman and man: the fantasmatic support of this ideal couple would have been the figure of *a frog embracing a bottle of beer*—an inconsistent figure that, instead of guaranteeing the harmony of the sexual relationship, renders palpable its ridiculous discord. (Of course, the obvious feminist point would be that what women witness in their everyday love experience is rather the opposite: one kisses a beautiful young man and, after one gets too close to him, that is, when it is already too late, one notices that he is effectively a frog.) This opens up the possibility of undermining the hold a fantasy exerts over us through the very over-identification with it: by way of embracing simultaneously, within the same space, the multitude of inconsistent fantasmatic elements. That is to say, each of the two subjects is involved in his or her own subjective fantasizing—the girl fantasizes about the frog who is really a young man, the man about the girl who is really a bottle of beer. What modern art and writing oppose to this is not objective reality but the "objectively subjective" underlying fantasy that the two subjects are never able to assume, something similar to a Magrittesque painting of a frog embracing a bottle of beer, with a title "A man and a woman" or "The ideal couple."[28]

IN THE VULGAR JOKE about a fool having intercourse for the first time, the girl has to tell him exactly what to do: "See this hole between my legs? Put it in here. Now push it deep. Now pull it out. Push it in, pull it out, push it in, pull it out ..." "Now wait a minute," the fool interrupts her, "make up your mind! In or out?"[29]

THERE IS A YUGOSLAV RIDDLE-JOKE: "What is the difference between the pope and a trumpet? The pope is from Rome, and the trumpet is [made] from tin. And what is the difference between the pope from Rome and the trumpet [made] from tin? The trumpet [made] from tin can be from Rome, while the pope from Rome cannot be [made] from tin." In a similar way, we should redouble the Parisian graffiti joke: "What is the difference between 'God is dead' and 'Nietzsche is dead'? It was Nietzsche who said 'God is dead,' and it was God who said 'Nietzsche is dead.' And what is the difference between Nietzsche, who said 'God is dead,' and God, who said 'Nietzsche is dead'? Nietzsche, who said 'God is dead,' was not dead, while the God who said 'Nietzsche is dead' *was himself dead*." Crucial for the proper comic effect is not a difference where we expect sameness but, rather, a sameness where we expect difference; this is why, as Alenka Zupančič has pointed out, the materialist (and therefore properly comic) version of the above joke would have been something like: "God is dead. And, as a matter of fact, I don't feel too well either …"[30]

THE MOMENT WE INTRODUCE the paradoxical dialectics of identity and similarity best exemplified by a series of Marx Brothers' jokes ("No wonder you look like X, since you *are* X!"; "This man may look like an idiot and act like an idiot, but don't let that fool you—he really is an idiot!"), the uncanniness of cloning becomes clear. Let us take the case of a beloved only child who dies, and the parents then decide to clone him and so get him back: is it not more than clear that the result is monstrous? The new child has all the properties of the dead one, *but this very similarity makes the difference all the more palpable*—although he looks exactly the same, he is not the same person, so he is a cruel joke, a terrifying impostor—not the lost son, but a blasphemous copy whose presence cannot fail to remind us of the old joke from the Marx Brothers' *Night at the Opera*: "Everything about you reminds me of you—your eyes, your throat, your lips, … everything *except you*!"[31]

FOR DECADES, A CLASSIC JOKE has been circulating among Lacanians to exemplify the key role of the Other's knowledge: a man who believes himself to be a kernel of grain is taken to a mental institution where the doctors do their best to convince him that he is not a kernel of grain but a man; however, when he is cured (convinced that he is not a kernel of grain but a man) and allowed to leave the hospital, he immediately comes back, trembling and very scared—there is a chicken outside the door, and he is afraid it will eat him. "My dear fellow," says his doctor, "you know very well that you are not a kernel of grain but a man." "Of course I know," replies the patient, "but does the chicken?"

Therein resides the true stake of psychoanalytic treatment: it is not enough to convince the patient about the unconscious truth of his symptoms; the unconscious itself must be brought to assume this truth. The same holds true for the Marxian theory of commodity fetishism: we can imagine a bourgeois subject attending a Marxism course where he is taught about commodity fetishism. After the course, he comes back to his teacher, complaining that he is still the victim of commodity fetishism. The teacher tells him "But you know now how things stand, that commodities are only expressions of social relations, that there is nothing magic about them!" to which the pupil replies: "Of course I know all that, but the commodities I am dealing with seem not to know it!" This is what Lacan aimed at in his claim that the true formula of materialism is not "God doesn't exist," but "God is unconscious."[32]

• This, at least, seems to be the predominant status of beliefs today, in our era that claims for itself the title "postideological." Niels Bohr, who already aptly answered Einstein's "God doesn't play dice" ("Don't tell God what to do!"), also provided the perfect example of how a fetishist disavowal of belief works in ideology: seeing a horseshoe on his door, the surprised visitor said that he doesn't believe in the superstition that it brings luck, to which Bohr snapped back: "I also do not believe in it; I have it there because I was told that it works even if one does not believe in it!"[33]

• So, again, the true task is not to convince the subject, but the chicken-commodities: not to change the way we speak about commodities, but *to change the way commodities speak among themselves.* Zupancic goes here to the end and imagines a brilliant example that refers to God himself: "In the enlightened society of, say, revolutionary terror, a man is put in prison because he believes in God. With different measures, but above all by means of an enlightened explanation, he is brought to the knowledge that God does not exist. When dismissed, the man comes running back, and explains how scared he is of being punished by God. Of course he knows that God does not exist, but does God also know that?"

It is in this precise sense that today's era is perhaps less atheist than any prior one: we are all ready to indulge in utter skepticism, cynical distance, exploitation of others "without any illusions," violations of all ethical constraints, extreme sexual practices, etc., etc.—protected by the silent awareness that the big Other is ignorant about it.[34]

- In the last years of President Tito's life, he was effectively such a chicken: some archives and memoirs show that, already in the mid-1970s, the leading figures around Tito were aware that Yugoslavia's economic situation was catastrophic; however, since Tito was nearing his death, they made a collective decision to postpone the outbreak of a crisis until his death—the price was the fast accumulation of external debt in the last years of Tito's life, when Yugoslavia was, to quote the rich bank client from Hitchcock's *Psycho*, buying off its unhappiness. When, in 1980, Tito finally died, the economic crisis did strike, leading to a 40 percent drop in the standard of living, to ethnic tensions and, finally, to civil and ethnic war that destroyed the country—the moment to confront the crisis adequately was missed. One can thus say that what put the last nail in the coffin of Yugoslavia was the very attempt by its leading circle to protect the ignorance of the leader, to keep his gaze happy.

THIS IS WHY "What is the difference between ..." jokes are most efficient when difference is denied, as in: "What is the difference between toy trains and women's breasts? None: both are meant for children, but it is mostly adult men that play with them."[35]

SIGNIFICANTLY, THE ONLY JOKE—or, if not a joke, then at least a moment of irony—in Heidegger occurs in his rather bad-taste quip about Lacan as "that psychiatrist who is himself in need of a psychiatrist" (in a letter to Medard Boss).[36]

THUS, SINCE THE BASIC TWIST OF THIS JOKE resides in the inclusion in the series of the apparent exception (the complaining patient is himself dying), its "negation" would have been a joke whose final twist would, on the contrary, involve exclusion from the series, that is to say, the extraction of the One, its positing as an exception to the series, as in a recent Bosnian joke in which Fata (the proverbial ordinary Bosnian wife) complains to a doctor that Muyo, her husband, makes love to her for hours every evening, so that, even in the darkness of their bedroom, she cannot get enough sleep—again and again, he jumps on her. The good doctor advises her to apply shock therapy: she should keep a bright lamp on her side of the bed, so that when she gets really tired of sex, she can suddenly illuminate Muyo's face; this shock is sure to cool his excessive passion. The same evening, after hours of sex, Fata does exactly as advised—and recognizes the face of Haso, one of Muyo's colleagues. Surprised, she asks him: "But what are you doing here? Where is Muyo, my husband?" The embarrassed Haso answers: "Well, last time I saw him he was there at the door, collecting money from those waiting in line." The third term here would be a kind of joke-correlative of "infinite judgment," tautology as supreme contradiction, as in the anecdote about a man who complains to his doctor that he often hears the voices of people who are not present with him in the room. The doctor replies: "Really? In order to enable me to discover the meaning of

this hallucination, could you describe to me in what precise circumstances you usually hear the voices of people
who are not with you?" "Well, it mostly happens when I
talk on the phone."[37]

THIS POINT BECOMES CLEARER through a particularly morbid joke. A patient in a large hospital room with many beds complains to the doctor about the constant noise that other patients are making, which is driving him crazy. The doctor replies that nothing can be done; one cannot forbid the patients from expressing their despair, since they all know they are dying. The first patient responds: "Why don't you then put them in a separate room for those who are dying?" The doctor replies calmly and glibly: "But this *is* a room for those who are dying."[38]

THERE IS ANOTHER KETTLE that the title of this book-
let aims at—the one from the joke evoked by Freud in
order to render the strange logic of dreams: (1) I never borrowed a kettle from you; (2) I returned it to you unbroken;
(3) the kettle was already broken when I got it from you.
Such an enumeration of inconsistent arguments, of course,
confirms *per negationem* what it endeavors to deny—that
I returned to you a broken kettle. Did the same inconsistency not characterize the justification of the attack on
Iraq in early 2003? (1) Saddam Hussein possesses weapons
of mass destruction that pose a "clear and present danger"
not only to his neighbors and Israel, but to all democratic
Western states. (2) So what to do when, in September 2003,
David Kay, the CIA official in charge of the search for
weapons of mass destruction (WMD) in Iraq, had to concede that no such weapons have so far been found (after
more than thousand US specialists spent months looking
for them)? One moves to the next level: even if Saddam
does not have any WMD, he was involved with al-Qaeda
in the 9/11 attack, so he should be punished as part of the
justified revenge for 9/11 and in order to prevent further
such attacks. (3) However, again, in September 2003, even
Bush had to concede: "We have no evidence that Saddam
Hussein was involved with the September 11 attacks." So
what to do after this painful concession, with regard to
the fact that a recent opinion poll found that nearly 70
percent of Americans believed the Iraqi leader was personally involved in the attacks? One moves to the next

level: even if there is no proof of the link with al-Qaeda, Saddam's regime is a ruthless dictatorial regime, a threat to its neighbors, and a catastrophe to its own people, and this fact alone provides reason enough to topple it. The problem, again, was that there were TOO MANY reasons for the attack.

Interestingly, Key himself offered three theories for the failure of finding the WMD: (1) the WMD are in Iraq; it is just that Saddam, the "master of deceit," hid them well; (2) the WMD are not in Iraq, because Saddam moved them outside the country just before the war; (3) Saddam never had them at all, and just bluffed to appear strong. (And, as a curiosity, there is an additional eccentric twist: Saddam's scientists were fooling Saddam himself, and were simply too afraid to tell him he didn't possess any weapons.)—And, incidentally, opponents of the war seemed to repeat the same inconsistent logic: (1) it is all really about the control of oil and American hegemony—the true rogue state that terrorizes others is the United States itself; (2) even if it is not only about oil and hegemony and the attack is justified, since Saddam is a murderer and torturer, and his regime a criminal catastrophe, it will be counterproductive—it will give a big boost to a new wave of anti-American terrorism; (3) even if successful, the attack on Iraq destined to overthrow Saddam will cost too much, and the money could be better spent elsewhere.[39]

VARIATION

- The joke evoked by Freud in order to render the strange logic of dreams gives us a useful gloss on the strange logic at work here: (1) I never borrowed a kettle from you; (2) I returned it to you unbroken; (3) the kettle was already broken when I got it from you. Such an enumeration of inconsistent arguments, of course, confirms by negation what it endeavors to deny—that I returned your kettle broken. Doesn't this very inconsistency characterize the way radical Islamists respond to the Holocaust? (1) The Holocaust did not happen. (2) It did happen, but the Jews deserved it. (3) The Jews did not deserve it, but they have lost the right to complain by doing to Palestinians what the Nazis did to them.[40]

IN THE EARLY DAYS of his government, Tony Blair liked to paraphrase the famous joke from Monty Python's *Life of Brian* ("All right, but apart from sanitation, medicine, education, wine, public order, irrigation, roads, the freshwater system, and public health, what have the Romans ever done for us?") in order ironically to disarm his critics: "They betrayed socialism. True, they brought more social security, they did a lot for healthcare and education, and so on, but, in spite of all that, they betrayed socialism."[41]

THE ULTIMATE EXAMPLE of this ambiguity is arguably the *chocolate laxative* available in the United States, with the paradoxical injunction "Do you have constipation? Eat more of this chocolate!" that is, the very thing that causes constipation. Do we not find here a weird version of Richard Wagner's famous line "Only the spear that caused the wound can heal it" from *Parsifal*? And is not a negative proof of the hegemony of this stance the fact that true unconstrained consumption (in all its main forms: drugs, free sex, smoking) is emerging as the main danger? The fight against these dangers is one of the main investments of today's "biopolitics." Solutions are desperately sought that would reproduce the paradox of the chocolate laxative. The main contender is "safe sex"—a term that makes one appreciative of the truth of the old saying "Is having sex with a condom not like taking a shower with a raincoat on?" The ultimate goal would be, along the lines of decaf coffee, to invent "opium without opium": no wonder marijuana is so popular among liberals who want to legalize it—it already IS a kind of "opium without opium."[42]

THERE IS THUS AN ELEMENT OF TRUTH in a joke about a young Christian girl's ideal prayer to the Virgin Mary: "O thou who conceived without having sinned, let me sin without having to conceive!"—in the perverse functioning of Christianity, religion is, in effect, evoked as a safeguard allowing us to enjoy life with impunity.[43]

WAS CHRIST, in effect, occupying the position of the son in the wonderful joke about the rabbi who turns in despair to God, asking him what he should do with his bad son, who has deeply disappointed him; God calmly answers: "Do the same as I did: write a new testament!"[44]

SUCH A FALL by means of which God loses his distance and becomes involved, steps into the human series, is discernible in a classic joke from the German Democratic Republic in which Richard Nixon, Leonid Brezhnev, and Erich Honecker confront God, asking him about the future of their countries. To Nixon, God answers: "In 2000, the United States will be Communist!" Nixon turns away and starts to cry. To Brezhnev, He says: "In 2000, the Soviet Union will be under Chinese control." After Brezhnev has also turned away and started to cry, Honecker finally asks: "And how will it be in my beloved GDR?" God turns away and starts to cry.

And here is the ultimate version: three Russians who share the same cell in Lubyanka prison have all been condemned for political offenses. While they are getting acquainted, the first says: "I was condemned to five years for opposing Popov." The second says: "Ah, but then the party line changed, and I was condemned to ten years for supporting Popov." Finally, the third one says: "I was condemned for life, and I *am* Popov."[45]

THIS ALSO MAKES MEANINGLESS the Christian joke according to which, when, in John 8:1–11, Christ says to those who want to stone the woman taken in adultery, "Let him who is without sin among you be the first to throw a stone!" he is immediately hit by a stone, and then shouts back: "Mother! I asked you to stay at home!"[46]

IN HIS BOOK ON JOKES, Freud refers to the story of a middleman who tries to convince a young man to marry a woman he represents; his strategy is to change every objection into something praiseworthy. When the man says "But the woman is ugly!" he answers, "So you will not have to worry that she will deceive you with others!" "She is poor!" "So she will be accustomed not to spend too much of your money!" and so on, until, finally, when the man formulates a reproach impossible to reinterpret in this way, the middleman explodes, "But what do you want? Perfection? Nobody is totally without faults!"

Would it not also be possible to discern in this joke the underlying structure of the legitimization of a Real Socialist regime? "There is not enough meat and rich food in the stores!" "So you don't have to worry about getting fat and suffering a heart attack!" "There are not enough interesting theatrical and cinema performances or good books available!" "Does this not enable you to cultivate all the more an intense social life, visiting friends and neighbors?" "The secret police exerts total control over my life!" "So you can just relax and lead a life safe from worries!" and so on, until … "But the air is so polluted from the nearby factory that all my children have life-threatening lung diseases!" "What do you want? No system is without faults!"[47]

VARIATION

•   In an old Soviet joke, a customer goes to a bank, announces his intention to deposit 100 rubles, and inquires about how safe the deposits are. The bank clerk tells him that the bank guarantees all deposits, but the customer asks: "What if the bank collapses?" The clerk answers that the central bank also guarantees all local banks and their deposits. The customer persists: but what if the central bank itself collapses? The clerk again replies: "Then the Soviet state guarantees all bank deposits!" Still unconvinced, the customer raises the stakes to the top: "But what if the Soviet state itself disintegrates?" To this, the bank clerk explodes: "Are you telling me that you are not ready to lose the lousy 100 rubles as the price for such a wonderful event as the disappearance of the Soviet Union!"

WOULD IT NOT BE POSSIBLE to retell, in this way, the elementary story of Christianity, namely, as a joke with the final unexpected twist? A believer is complaining, "I was promised contact with God, divine grace, but now I am totally alone, abandoned by God, destitute, suffering, with only a miserable death awaiting me!" The divine voice then answers him, "You see, now you are effectively one with God—with Christ suffering on the cross!"[48]

RECALL THIS JOKE that perfectly renders the logic of the (in)famous Hegelian triad: Three friends have a drink at a bar; the first one says, "A horrible thing happened to me. At my travel agency, I wanted to say 'A ticket to Pittsburgh!' and I said 'A picket to Tittsburgh!'" The second one replies, "That's nothing. At breakfast, I wanted to say to my wife 'Could you pass me the sugar, honey?' and what I said was 'You dirty bitch, you ruined my entire life!'" The third one concludes, "Wait till you hear what happened to me. After gathering my courage all night, I decided to say to my wife at breakfast exactly what you said to yours, and I ended up saying 'Could you pass me the sugar, honey?'"[49]

A COMIC HEGELIAN INTERLUDE:
DUMB AND DUMBER

How many people noticed that Hegelian dialectics is unconsciously practiced by Dan Quayle and George W. Bush? We thought we had seen it all with Quayle two decades ago; however, in comparison with Bush, Quayle emerges as a rather intelligent person. With regard to his famous mistake of correcting the spelling of "potato" into "potatoe," I myself must admit it always seemed to me that Quayle was somehow right: "potatoe" comes closer to what Humboldt would have called the true "inner form" of potato. (Nonetheless, I must admit that I feel something similar apropos of Bush's recent "Grecians" instead of "Greeks": "Keep good relations with the Grecians." "Grecian" does seem somehow more dignified, like "thou art" instead of "you are," while "Greek" sounds all too close to "geek"—were the founders of our noble Western civilization really just a bunch of geeks?)

How, then, does Bush compare with Quayle? Are Bush's slips, like those of Quayle at his best, at the level of the Marx Brothers' supreme slips ("No wonder you remind me of Emanuel Ravelli, since you ARE Ravelli!"), or of no less ingenious "goldwynisms," the sayings attributed to the larger-than-life Hollywood producer Sam Goldwyn (from "An oral agreement isn't worth the paper it's written on!" to the notorious "Include me out!")? Most of Quayle's and Bush's slips follow the basic formula of what the French call *lapalissades*, the tautological statings of the obvious attributed to the mythical figure of Monsieur la Palice, like "One hour before his death, Monsieur la Palice was still fully alive." Indeed, la Palice's ingenious "Why don't we build cities in the countryside where the air is much cleaner?" comes pretty close to a concise formulation of the Republican Party's ecological policy, rendered perfectly by Bush's truism: "I know the human being and fish can coexist peacefully."

Here, then, are some examples of this elementary type of slip from Bush and Quayle: "If we don't succeed, we run the risk of failure"; "A low voter turnout is an indication of fewer people going to the polls"; "For NASA, space is still a high priority." These *lapalissades* get a little bit more interesting when pure tautology is emphatically offered as a causal explanation; see the following slip of Quayle: "When I have been asked who caused the riots and the killing in Los Angeles, my answer has been direct and simple: Who is to blame for the riots? The rioters are to blame. Who is to blame for the killings? The killers are to blame." (There is, of course, an implicit conservative political logic in this tautology, that is, this quote relies on an implicit negation: don't look for the "deeper" causes in social circumstances, it is the immediate perpetrators who bear the full responsibility.) Things get even more interesting when, in a strangely Hegelian way, Quayle explodes the identity by opposing the notion and its empirical exemplifications: "It isn't pollution that's harming the environment. It's the impurities in our air and water that are doing it."

While Bush is not able to follow Quayle along this road, he often does catch up with him in producing slips in which a conceptual opposition is raised to the level of dialectical self-relating *Selbstbeziehung*. Recall how he posited the very opposition between irreversibility and reversibility as reversible: "I believe we are on an irreversible trend towards more freedom and democracy—but that could change." So it's not simply that things are either reversible or irreversible: a situation that appears irreversible could change into a reversible one. Here is an even nicer example of this reflexivity: "The future will be better tomorrow." The point is not simply that Quayle made a mistake, intending to claim that tomorrow things will be better: in the near future (tomorrow), *future itself* will look brighter to us. Did Bush not reproduce exactly the same structure in his statement "One of the common denominators I have found is that expectations rise above that which is expected"?

With Quayle, this reflexivity culminates in the following quote in which the series of three evasions/disavowals is consummated in the speaker's self-erasure from the picture: "The Holocaust was an obscene period in our nation's history. I mean in this century's history. But we all lived in this century. I didn't live in this century." The logic of progress in this series is inexorable: first, in his eagerness to square the accounts with the dark past of his own nation, Quayle attributes to it the crime of the century that it did NOT commit; then he retracts, specifying that the act was not committed by his nation; in a desperate attempt to return to the logic of settling the accounts with one's past, he then constitutes a new community—no longer "our nation," but all of us who lived in the last century and are thus coresponsible for the Holocaust; finally, becoming aware of the mess he talked himself into, he as it were automatically opts for a quick escape, excluding himself from his own century. In short, in a gesture that forms the perfect reversal of Goldwyn's "include me out," Quayle "excludes himself in" his century! No wonder, then, that, after this imbroglio, he makes a statement that provides the most succinct characterization of Bush: "People that are really weird can get into sensitive positions and have a tremendous impact on history."

There are, however, two domains in which Bush goes further than Quayle; the first is that of the postmodern dialectics of certainty and uncertainty. In Bush's thought, uncertainty (about the empirical figure of the enemy), far from diminishing the danger, dialectically inverts itself into the higher certainty that there MUST BE an enemy, all the more dangerous for the fact that we don't know who, exactly, he is. So the more uncertainty about the enemy, the more we can be certain of him lurking out there: "This is a world that is much more uncertain than the past. In the past we were certain, we were certain it was us versus the Russians in the past. We were certain, and therefore we had huge nuclear arsenals aimed at each other to keep peace. … Even though it's an uncertain world, we're certain of some things. … We're certain there are madmen in this world, and there's terror, and there's missiles and I'm certain of this too." Bush also surpasses Quayle with regard to the refined reflexive twist of the simple Christian precept "Love your neighbor like yourself!" Bush took the lesson of the dialectics of the desire for recognition from Hegel's *Phenomenology of Spirit*: we do not directly love ourselves—what we effectively love is to be loved by others, that is, we love others to love us: "We must all hear the universal call to like your neighbor just like you like to be liked yourself."

So what should the unfortunate Bush do to avoid Quayle's sad fate and to dispel the blindness of the stupid liberal public, which is unable to appreciate the hidden dialectical finesse of his statements? As we all know, not only is it true that *du sublime au ridicule, il n'y a qu'un pas*; the same goes also the other way round. So, perhaps, Bush should just learn the Heideggerian art of generating deep insights from tautological reversals. That is to say, when we recall Heidegger's famous reversal "*das Wesen der Wahrheit ist die Wahrheit des Wesens* [the essence of truth is the truth of the essence]," or his rhetorical strategy of excluding *das Wesen* of some domain from this domain itself ("the essence of technology is nothing technological"), it cannot but strike us how easy it would have been to change some bushism into a deep thought. "This is Preservation Month. I appreciate preservation. It's what you do when you run for president. You gotta preserve" could be translated into: "The essence of preservation has nothing to do with the ontic preservation of our physical resources. The essence of preservation is the preservation of the essence of our society itself—and this is what the president of the United States has to do, even if, at the vulgar ontic level, he allows the destruction of more natural resources than in the entire previous history of the United States."

In learning this art, Bush will regain a chance of proving himself a worthy successor to Bill Clinton, since this Heideggerian trend in the American presidency was discernible already in the Clinton era: when Clinton answered the prosecutor's question about his relationship with Monica Lewinsky ("Is it true that …?") with the infamous "It depends on what you mean by 'is,'" was he not pointing toward the Heideggerian *Seinsfrage*?[50]

RECALL THE CLASSIC GROUCHO MARX LINE: "This man may look like an idiot and act like an idiot, but don't let that fool you—he really is an idiot!" Is the denouement of Hitchcock's *Vertigo* not a version of this joke? "This woman (Judy) may look like Madeleine and act like Madeleine, but don't let that fool you—she really is Madeleine!"[51]

VARIATION

- Recall the often quoted Marx Brothers joke about Ravelli: *Spaulding:* Say, I used to know a fellow looked exactly like you, by the name of ... ah ... Emanuel Ravelli. Are you his brother? *Ravelli:* I'm Emanuel Ravelli. *Spaulding:* You're Emanuel Ravelli? *Ravelli:* I'm Emanuel Ravelli. *Spaulding:* Well, no wonder you look like him ... But I still insist, there is a resemblance.[52]

TODAY, THE OLD JOKE ABOUT A RICH MAN telling his servant "Throw out this destitute beggar—I'm so sensitive that I can't stand seeing people suffer!" is more appropriate than ever.[53]

IN AN OLD JOKE from the defunct German Democratic Republic, a German worker gets a job in Siberia; aware of how all mail will be read by censors, he tells his friends: "Let's establish a code: if a letter you will get from me is written in ordinary blue ink, it is true; if it is written in red ink, it is false." After a month, his friends get the first letter, written in blue ink: "Everything is wonderful here: stores are full, food is abundant, apartments are large and properly heated, movie theaters show films from the West, there are many beautiful girls ready for an affair—the only thing unavailable is *red ink*."

And is this not our situation till now? We have all the freedoms one wants—the only thing missing is the "red ink": we "feel free" because we lack the very language to articulate our unfreedom. What this lack of red ink means is that, today, all the main terms we use to designate the present conflict—"war on terror," "democracy and freedom," "human rights," etc.—are false terms, mystifying our perception of the situation instead of allowing us to think it. The task today is to give the protesters red ink.[54]

IN A CLASSIC LINE from a Hollywood screwball comedy, the girl asks her boyfriend: "Do you want to marry me?" "No!" "Stop dodging the issue! Give me a straight answer!" In a way, the underlying logic is correct: the only acceptable straight answer for the girl is "Yes!" so anything else, inclusive of a straight "No!" counts as evasion. This underlying logic, of course, is again that of the forced choice: you are free to decide, on condition that you make the right choice. Would a priest not rely on the same paradox in a dispute with a skeptic layman? "Do you believe in God?" "No." "Stop dodging the issue! Give me a straight answer!" Again, in the eyes of the priest, the only straight answer is to assert one's belief in God: far from standing for a symmetrical clear stance, the atheist denial of belief is an attempt to dodge the issue of the divine encounter. And is it not the same today with the choice "democracy or fundamentalism"? Is it not that, within the terms of this choice, it is simply not possible to choose "fundamentalism"? What is problematic in the way the ruling ideology imposes on us this choice is not "fundamentalism" but, rather, *democracy itself*: as if the only alternative to "fundamentalism" is the political system of the parliamentary liberal democracy.[55]

THERE IS AN ISRAELI JOKE about Bill Clinton visiting Bibi Netanyahu: when Clinton sees a mysterious blue phone in Bibi's office, he asks Bibi what it is, and Bibi answers that it allows him to dial Him up there in the sky. Upon his return to the States, the envious Clinton demands that his secret service should provide him with such a phone—at any cost. They deliver it within two weeks, and it works, but the phone bill is exorbitant—two million dollars for a one-minute talk with Him up there. So Clinton furiously calls Bibi and complains: "How can you afford such a phone, if even we, who support you financially, can't? Is this how you spend our money?" Bibi answers calmly: "No, it's not that—you see, for us, Jews, that call counts as a local call!"

Interestingly, in the Soviet version of the joke, God is replaced by hell: when Nixon visits Brezhnev and sees a special phone, Brezhnev explains to him that this is a link to hell; at the end of the joke, when Nixon complains about the price of the call, Brezhnev calmly answers: "For us in the Soviet Union, the call to hell counts as a local call."[56]

ONE SHOULD THEREFORE ASSUME the paradox that concentration camps and refugee camps for the delivery of humanitarian aid are the two faces, "human" and "inhuman," of the same socio-logical formal matrix. In both cases, the cruel joke from Lubitch's *To Be or Not to Be* applies: when asked about the German concentration camps in the occupied Poland, the character called "Concentration Camp Erhardt" snaps back "We do the concentrating, and the Poles do the camping." (And does the same not hold for the Enron bankruptcy in January 2002, which can be interpreted as a kind of ironic commentary on the notion of risk society? Thousands of employees who lost their jobs and savings were certainly exposed to a risk, but without any true choice—the risk appeared to them as blind fate. Those, on the contrary, who effectively did have an insight into the risks as well as a possibility to intervene into the situation [the top managers], minimized their risks by cashing in their stocks and options before the bankruptcy—actual risks and choices were thus nicely distributed. So, again, apropos of the popular notion that today's society is that of risky choices, one can say that some [the Enron managers] do the choices, while others [the common employees] do the risking.)[57]

IN ONE OF THE FUNNIEST SCENES in *To Be or Not to Be*, the pretentious Polish actor Josef Tura who, as the part of a secret mission, has to impersonate the cruel high Gestapo officer Erhardt, does this impersonation in an exaggerated way, reacting to the remarks of his interlocutor about his cruel treatment of the Poles with a loud vulgar laughter and a satisfied reply, "So they call me Concentration Camp Erhardt, hahaha!" We, the spectators, see this as a ridiculous caricature—however, a little bit later, Tura has to escape and the real Erhardt arrives; when the conversation again touches rumors about him, he reacts to his interlocutors *in exactly the same ridiculously exaggerated way* as his impersonator did. The message is clear: even Ehrhardt himself is not immediately himself, he also imitates his own copy or, more precisely, the ridiculous idea of himself. While Tura acts him, Erhardt acts himself.

In Hitchcock's *Vertigo*, we find a more tragic version of the same uncanny coincidence: the low-class Judy who, under the pressure exerted by Scottie and out of her love for him, endeavors to look and act like the high-class and ethereal Madeleine, turns out to BE Madeleine: they are the same person, since the "true" Madeleine Scottie encountered was already a fake. However, this identity of Judy and Judy-Madeleine again renders all the more palpable the absolute otherness of Madeleine with regard to Judy—the Madeleine that is given nowhere, who is present just in the guise of the ethereal "aura" that envelops Judy-Madeleine.[58]

JEREMY BENTHAM deployed the unique notion of "self-icon," that is, the notion that a thing is its own best sign (as in the Lewis Carroll joke about Englishmen using ever larger maps, until they finally settled on using England itself as *its own map*).[59]

IN SO FAR AS THE MELANCHOLIC MOURNS what he has not yet lost, there is an inherent comic subversion of the tragic procedure of mourning at work in melancholy, as in the old racist joke about gypsies: when it rains, they are happy because they know that after rain there is always sunshine; when the sun shines, they feel sad because they know that after sunshine it will, at some point, rain.[60]

IN AN OLD SOVIET JOKE, a listener asks Radio Erevan: "Did Rabinovitch win a new car in the state lottery?" Radio Erevan replies: "In principle, yes—he did. Only it was not a car but a bicycle, it was not new but old, and he did not win it, it was stolen from him!"[61]

THERE IS AN OLD RACIST JOKE, popular in the former Yugoslavia, about a gypsy being examined by a psychiatrist. The psychiatrist first explains to the gypsy what free associations are: you immediately say what is on your mind in response to the psychiatrist's cue. Then the psychiatrist proceeds to the test itself: he says "table"; the gypsy answers: "fucking Fatima"; he says "sky"; the gypsy answers: "fucking Fatima," and so on, until the psychiatrist explodes: "But you didn't understand me! You must tell me what crops up in your mind, what you are thinking of, when I say my word!" The gypsy calmly answers: "Yes, I got your point, I'm not stupid, but I think *all the time* about fucking Fatima!"[62]

THIS JOKE, which clearly displays the structure of Hegelian "abstract universality," has none the less to be supplemented by the crucial final twist at work in another joke about a pupil being examined by his biology teacher about different animals, and always reducing the answer to the definition of a horse: "What is an elephant?" "An animal that lives in the jungle, where there are no horses. A horse is a domestic mammal with four legs, used for riding, working in the fields or pulling vehicles." "What is a fish?" "An animal that has no legs, unlike a horse. A horse is a domestic mammal ..." "What is a dog?" "An animal that, unlike horses, barks. A horse is a domestic mammal ..." and so forth, until finally, the desperate teacher asks the pupil: "OK, what is a *horse*?" Perplexed and totally thrown off balance, the poor surprised pupil starts to mumble and cry, unable to provide an answer.[63]

JOKES ABOUT THE CROATIAN PRESIDENT Franjo Tudjman in general display a structure of some interest for Lacanian theory—for example: Why is it impossible to play "hide-and-seek" with Tudjman? Because if he were to hide, nobody would bother to seek him ... a nice libidinal point about how hiding works only if people actually want to find you. But the supreme example is that of Tudjman and his large family in a plane above Croatia. Aware of the rumors that a lot of Croats lead miserable, unhappy lives, while he and his cronies amass wealth, Tudjman says: "What if I were to throw a check for a million dollars out of the window, to make at least one Croat, who will catch it, happy?" His flattering wife says: "But Franjo, my dear, why don't you throw out two checks for half a million each, and thus make two Croats happy?" His daughter adds: "Why not four checks for a quarter of a million each, and make four Croats happy?" and so on, until finally, his grandson—the proverbial innocent youth who unknowingly blurts out the truth—says: "But Grandpa, why don't you simply throw yourself out of the window, and thus make *all* the Croats happy?"[64]

THERE IS A STANDARD SERBO-CROAT vulgar riddle-joke: "How do you make eggs on the eye? By putting a cock on the forehead!" (In Slavic languages, the vulgar term for testicles is eggs, not balls.) It accounts for the scene I witnessed in the barracks: after a particularly tasteless dinner, which was left uneaten by most of the soldiers, the unfortunate soldier, lying on his bed, the victim of a practical joke, loudly complained that he was still very hungry and wouldn't mind a simple meal, perhaps a pair of eggs on the eye; his fellow soldiers immediately seized the opportunity and provided him with "eggs on the eye" by putting a cock on his forehead.[65]

IN THE GOOD OLD DAYS of "actually existing Socialism," every schoolchild was told again and again of how Lenin read voraciously, and of his advice to young people: "Learn, learn, and learn!" A classic joke from Socialism produces a nice subversive effect by using this motto in an unexpected context. Marx, Engels, and Lenin were each asked what they preferred, a wife or a mistress. Marx, whose attitude in intimate matters is well known to have been rather conservative, answered "A wife"; Engels, who knew how to enjoy life, answered, of course, "A mistress"; the surprise comes with Lenin, who answered "Both, wife *and* mistress!" Is he dedicated to a hidden pursuit of excessive sexual pleasures? No, since he quickly explains: "This way, you can tell your mistress that you're with your wife, and your wife that you are about to visit your mistress ..." "And what do you actually do?" "I go to a solitary place and learn, learn, and learn!"[66]

TWO VULGAR JOKES about testicles from Eastern Europe illustrate the fool-knave opposition perfectly. In the first one, a customer is sitting at a bar, drinking whisky; a monkey comes dancing along the counter, stops at his glass, washes his balls in it, and dances away. Badly shocked, the customer orders another glass of whisky; the monkey strolls along again and does the same. Furious, the customer asks the bartender: "Do you know why that monkey is washing his balls in my whisky?" The bartender replies: "I have no idea—ask the gypsy, he knows everything!" The guest turns to the gypsy, who is wandering around the bar, amusing guests with his violin and songs, and asks him: "Do you know why that monkey is washing his balls in my whisky?" The gypsy answers calmly: "Yes, sure!" and starts to sing a sad melancholic song: "Why does that monkey wash his balls in my whisky, oh why …" The point, of course, is that gypsy musicians are supposed to know hundreds of songs and perform them at the customers' request, so the gypsy has understood the customer's question as a request for a song about a monkey washing his balls in whisky. This is the poetry of ideology at its purest.

The second joke takes place in fourteenth-century Russia under Mongol occupation. A peasant and his wife were walking along a dusty country road; a Mongol warrior on a horse stopped at their side and told the peasant he would now proceed to rape his wife; he then added: "But since there is a lot of dust on the ground, you must hold my testicles while I rape your wife, so that they will not get dirty!" Once the Mongol had done the deed and ridden away, the peasant started laughing and jumping with joy. His surprised wife asked: "How can you be jumping with joy when I was just brutally raped in your presence?" The farmer answered: "But I got him! His balls are covered with dust!" This sad joke tells of the predicament of dissidents: they thought they were dealing serious blows to the party *nomenklatura* (the representatives of ordinary people), but all they were doing was getting a little bit of dust on the *nomenklatura*'s testicles, while the *nomenklatura* went on raping the people. Is today's critical Left not in a similar position? (Among today's terms for softly smearing with dust the balls of those in power are "deconstruction" and "protection of individual freedoms.") In a famous confrontation at the university of Salamanca in 1936, Miguel de Unamuno quipped at Franquists: *"Venceréis, pero no convenceréis"* ("You will win, but you will not convince"). Is this all that today's Left can say to triumphant global capitalism? Is the Left predestined to continue to play the role of those who, on the contrary, convince but fail (and are especially convincing in retroactively explaining the reasons for their own failure)? Our task is to discover how to make a step further—our thesis 11 should be: in our societies, critical Leftists have hitherto only dirtied with dust the balls of those in power; the point is to cut them off.[67]

TAKE THE OLD JOKE about the difference between Soviet-style bureaucratic Socialism and Yugoslav self-management Socialism: in Russia, members of the *nomenklatura* drive themselves in expensive limousines, while in Yugoslavia, *ordinary people themselves ride in limousines through their representatives.*[68]

UNDOUBTEDLY THE GREATEST MASTERS of humor in cinema (as opposed to the Marx Brothers' jokes) are the members of Monty Python. An episode from their *Meaning of Life* takes place in a couple's apartment. Two men from the "live organ transplants" business ring the bell and demand the husband's liver. The poor husband resists: they have the right to take his liver only in the event of his death; but the two men assure him that in any case he is not likely to survive the removal of his liver.

The two men set to work, dragging bloody organs out of the victim's viscera with cold indifference. The wife cannot stand the sight and leaves the room for the kitchen; one of the men follows her and demands her liver too. She refuses; however, a gentleman then steps out of the refrigerator singing about the billions of stars and planets, and their intelligent dispositions within the universe. After she realizes how small and insignificant her problem is compared to the universe, she gladly agrees to donate her liver.[69]

THIS INHERENT REFERENCE to the Other on account of which "there is no Don Giovanni without Leporello" (Don Giovanni obviously rates the inscription of his conquests into Leporello's register higher than the pleasure provided by the conquests themselves) is the theme of a low-class joke on a poor peasant who, after surviving a shipwreck, finds himself on a desert island with Cindy Crawford. After having sex with her, she asks him if he is fully satisfied; his answer is yes, but none the less he still has a small request to make his satisfaction complete—could she dress herself up as his best friend, put on trousers, and paint a mustache on her face? In response to her surprised reaction and suspicion that the poor peasant is a hidden pervert, he comforts her that this is not the point at all, as she will immediately see. So, after she fulfills his request, he approaches her, elbows her in the ribs and tells her, with the obscene smile of the male complicity: "You know what just happened to me? I just had sex with Cindy Crawford!"[70]

AS DELEUZE EMPHASIZED, the stupid joke about a masochist asking a sadist to beat him up cruelly, and the sadist answering him with a malicious smile: "No, never ... ," completely misses the point: the relationship between sadism and masochism is not complementary; that is to say, the sadist and the masochist definitely do not form an ideal couple; their relationship is definitely not a relationship in which each of the two partners gets from the other what he wants (in which the masochist's pain is directly the sadist's satisfaction, and vice versa).[71]

IN ONE OF HIS LETTERS, Freud refers to the joke about the new husband who, asked by his friend how his wife looks, how beautiful she is, answers: "I personally don't like her, but that's a matter of taste."[72]

HITCHCOCK TELLS the joke that gave the name to the object called a McGuffin, which is actually a "strangers-on-a-train" joke. It also has a Yugoslav version with an alternate ending:

"What is the package on the rack?"

"It's a McGuffin."

"What is it for?"

"To kill the lions in the Highlands."

"But there are no lions in the Highlands."

Punchline A: "Well, then, that's no McGuffin."

Punchline B: "You see, it works."[73]

THE HEGELIAN SUBJECT emerges precisely by way of the reflective, self-relating, reapplication of a logical operator, as in the worn-out joke about the cannibal who ate the last cannibal in the tribe.[74]

ONE OF THE CONCLUSIONS to be drawn from this is that, in endeavoring to provide an answer to the question "Why were Jews specifically picked out to play the scapegoat role in anti-Semitic ideology?" we might easily succumb to the very trap of anti-Semitism, looking for some mysterious feature in them that, as it were, predestined them for that role: the fact that Jews who were chosen for the role of the "Jew" ultimately is contingent—as it is pointed out by the joke about anti-Semitism: "Jews and cyclists are responsible for all our troubles.—Why cyclists?—WHY JEWS?"[75]

ITS UNDERLYING MECHANISM was elaborated by
Michel Pêcheux apropos of jokes of the type: "Daddy was
born in Manchester, Mummy in Bristol, and I in London;
strange that the three of us should have met!"[76]

SUCH AN UNDERSTANDING OF HEGEL inevitably runs counter to the accepted notion of "absolute knowledge" as a monster of conceptual totality devouring every contingency; this Hegelian commonplace simply *shoots too fast*, like the patrolling soldier in the joke from Jaruzelski's Poland immediately after the military coup. At that time, military patrols had the right to shoot without warning at people walking on the streets after curfew (ten o'clock). One of the two soldiers on patrol sees somebody in a hurry at ten minutes to ten and immediately shoots him. When his colleague asks him why he shot when it was only ten to ten, he answers: "I knew the fellow—he lived far from here and in any case would not be able to reach his home in ten minutes, so to simplify matters, I shot him now."[77]

THE POINT IS, AS LACAN PUTS IT, that the emperor is naked only beneath his clothes, so if there is an unmasking gesture of psychoanalysis, it is closer to Alphonse Allais's joke, quoted by Lacan: somebody points at a woman and utters a horrified cry, "Look at her—what a shame, under her clothes, she is totally naked!"[78]

THERE IS A VERY HEGELIAN JOKE that illustrates perfectly the way truth arises from misrecognition—the way our path toward truth coincides with the truth itself. At the beginning of this century, a Pole and a Jew were sitting in a train, facing each other. The Pole was shifting nervously, watching the Jew all the time; something was irritating him. Finally, unable to restrain himself any longer, he exploded: "Tell me, how do you Jews succeed in extracting from people the last small coin and in this way accumulate all your wealth?" The Jew replied: "OK, I will tell you, but not for nothing; first, you give me five zloty [Polish money]." After receiving the required amount, the Jew began: "First, you take a dead fish; you cut off her head and put her entrails in a glass of water. Then, around midnight, when the moon is full, you must bury this glass in a churchyard ..." "And," the Pole interrupted him greedily, "if I do all this, will I also become rich?" "Not too quickly: replied the Jew; "This is not all you must do; but if you want to hear the rest, you must pay me another five zloty!" After receiving the additional money, the Jew continued his story; soon afterward, he again demanded more money, and so on, until finally the Pole exploded in fury: "You dirty rascal, do you really think I did not notice what you were aiming at? There is no secret at all, you simply want to extract the last small coin from me!" The Jew answered him calmly and with resignation: "Well, now you see how we, the Jews …"[79]

VARIATION

- Let us recall here the joke about a Jew and a Pole in which the Jew extracts money from the Pole under the pretext of imparting to him the secret of how Jews succeed in extracting from people their very last penny. Weininger's violent antifeminist outburst—"There is no feminine secret at all; behind the mask of the Enigma, there is simply nothing!"—remains at the level of the Pole's fury, which wells up when he finally grasps how the Jew, by endlessly postponing the final revelation, was merely extracting more and more money from him. What Weininger fails to do is make a gesture that would correspond to the Jew's answer to the Pole's outburst: "Well, now you see how we, the Jews, extract money from people …"—that is, a gesture that would reinterpret, reinscribe, the failure as a success—something like "Look, this nothingness behind the mask is the very absolute negativity on account of which woman is the subject *par excellence*, not a limited object opposed to the force of subjectivity!"[80]

ANOTHER JOKE POSSESSES exactly the same structure, but this is usually overlooked—we are referring to the joke about the Door of the Law from the ninth chapter of Kafka's *Trial*, to its final turnaround when the dying man from the country asks the doorkeeper: "Everyone strives to attain the law; how does it come about, then, that in all these years no one has come seeking admittance but me?" The doorkeeper perceives that the man is at the end of his strength and his hearing is failing, so he bellows in his ear: "No one but you could gain admittance through this door, since the door was intended only for you. I am now going to shut it."[81]

We could even invent another ending for Kafka's story to bring it nearer to the joke about the Pole and the Jew: after the long wait, the man from the country breaks out in fury and begins to cry at the doorkeeper: "You dirty rascal, why do you pretend to guard the entrance to some enormous secret, when you know very well that there is no secret beyond the door, that this door is intended only for me, to capture my desire!" and the doorkeeper (if he were an analyst) would answer him calmly: "You see, now you've discovered the real secret: beyond the door is only what your desire introduces there."[82]

THE LACANIAN "TITLE OF THE LETTER" is closer to the title of a picture; for example, that described in a joke about "Lenin in Warsaw." At an art exhibition in Moscow, there is a picture showing Nadezhda Krupskaya, Lenin's wife, in bed with a young member of the Komsomol. The title of the picture is "Lenin in Warsaw." A bewildered visitor asks a guide: "But where is Lenin?" The guide replies quietly and with dignity: "Lenin is in Warsaw."[83]

IF THE JOKE ABOUT LENIN IN WARSAW exemplifies the logic of the master-signifier, there is another joke—in a way its symmetrical inversion—that exemplifies the logic of the object: the joke about the conscript who tries to evade military service by pretending to be mad. His symptom is that he compulsively checks all the pieces of paper he can lay his hands on, constantly repeating: "That is not it!" He is sent to the military psychiatrist, in whose office he also examines all the papers around, including those in the wastepaper basket, repeating all the time: "That is not it!" The psychiatrist, finally convinced that he really is mad, gives him a written warrant releasing him from military service. The conscript casts a look at it and says cheerfully: "That *is* it!"

The Lacanian *objet a* is such a paradoxical entity that emerges as the result of the subject's search for it.[84]

THAT IS WHY IT CAN BE ILLUSTRATED by a multitude of jokes based on the same matrix: "Is this the place where the Duke of Wellington spoke his famous words?" "Yes, this is the place, but he never spoke those words." These never-spoken words are a Lacanian Real. One can quote examples *ad infinitum*: "Smith not only doesn't believe in ghosts; he isn't even afraid of them!" ... up to God himself who, according to Lacan, belongs to the Real: "God has all perfections except one—he doesn't exist!"[85]

IT IS LIKE THE SOVIET JOKE about Rabinovitch, a Jew who wants to emigrate. The bureaucrat at the emigration office asks him why; Rabinovitch answers: "There are two reasons why. The first is that I'm afraid that in the Soviet Union the Communists will lose power, there will be a counterrevolution, and the new power will put all the blame for the Communist crimes on us, Jews—there will again be anti-Jewish pogroms ..." "But," interrupts the bureaucrat, "this is pure nonsense, nothing can change in the Soviet Union, the power of the Communists will last forever!" "Well," responds Rabinovitch calmly, "that's my second reason."[86]

VARIATIONS

- The structure of this reconciliation in mature Hegel is, again, that of the joke on Rabinovitch: "There are two reasons modern society is reconciled with itself. The first is the interaction of civil society ..." "But the civil society interaction is a constant strife, the very mechanism of disintegration, of ruthless competition!" "Well, this is the second reason, since this very strife and competition makes individuals thoroughly interdependent and thus generates the ultimate social link."[87]

- Are we here not back at the structure of the Rabinovitch joke? "Why do you think you are exploited?" "For two reasons. First, when I work, the capitalist appropriates my surplus value." "But you are now unemployed; no one is appropriating your surplus value because you create none!" "That is the second reason." Everything hinges here on the fact that the capitalist totality of production not only needs workers, but also generates the "reserve army" of those who cannot find work: the latter are not simply outside the circulation of capital, they are actively produced as not-working by this circulation. Or, to refer again to the *Ninotchka* joke, they are not simply not-working, their not-working is their positive feature in the same way as "coffee without milk" is its positive feature.[88]

· So, to retell the experience in the terms of the Rabinovitch joke: "We are going to Jerusalem for two reasons. First, we want to find Christ's tomb, to dwell in the presence of divinity." "But what you will discover in Jerusalem is that the tomb is empty, that there is nothing to find there, that all you have is yourself, Christians who are there." "Well, this community of spirit IS the living Christ, and this is what we were really looking for!" The same goes for resurrection itself: "Christ will be resurrected!" "But we, his followers, who are waiting for him, we see nothing." "True, you don't see— what you don't see is that the spirit of this community of yours, the love that bonds you, IS the resurrected Christ!" And the same goes even more for the entire topic of the Second Coming: nothing will "really happen," no miracle of a God appearing, people will just realize that God IS ALREADY HERE, in the Spirit of their collective.[89]

· An unexpected version of the Rabinovitch joke was circulating in the former Yugoslavia: an officer wants to educate a gypsy soldier by teaching him poetry; so, in order to explain to him what rhyme is, he gives an example: "I play the balalaika, and I screw your mother." (In Serb, this line rhymes: *Igram balalaiku, yebem tvoiu maiku.*) The gypsy answers: "Oh, I got it! Here is another one: I play the balalaika, I screw your wife." The officer comments: "But this is not a rhyme!" The gypsy retorts: "It is not a rhyme, but it is true." The catch is that, in Serbian, this last line loosely rhymes (*Nije rima, ali je istina*), so that we finally do get a rhyme, but as a second answer to the officer's reaction to the first answer which was wrong (providing no rhyme).[90]

- This is what Hegel deployed as the dialectical shift in which the predicate itself turns into the subject—a shift that, again, can be retold as a version of the Rabinovitch joke: "I found the essence of femininity." "But one cannot find it, femininity is dispersed, displaced." "Well, this dispersion IS the essence of femininity."[91]

- Today, however, Jews effectively fear that, with the disintegration of communism and the emergence of nationalistic forces openly advocating anti-Semitism, the blame will again be put on them, so that today we can easily imagine the reversal of the joke, with Rabinovitch answering the bureaucrat's question: "There are two reasons why. The first is that I know that communism in Russia will last forever, nothing will really change here, and this prospect is unbearable for me." "But," interrupts the bureaucrat, "this is pure nonsense, communism's crimes will be severely punished!" "That's my second reason!" responds Rabinovitch.[92]

A PHENOMENON CAN THUS tell the truth precisely by presenting itself as a lie, like the Jew in the Freudian joke often quoted by Lacan who reproaches his friend: "Why are you telling me that you are going to Cracow and not to Lemberg, when you're really going to Cracow?" (Telling the truth represented a breach of the implicit code of deception that ruled their relationship: when one of them was going to Cracow, he was supposed to tell the lie that his destination was Lemberg, and vice versa).[93]

VARIATIONS

- The elementary semantic axis that legitimizes party rule is the opposition between self-managing social-ism and "bureaucratic" state-and-party socialism—in other words, the party-and-state bureaucracy legiti-mizes its rule by an ideology which designates *itself* as the principal enemy, so that an ordinary Yugoslav sub-ject could address to the ruling bureaucracy the same question as was addressed by one Jew to another in the joke recounted earlier. "Why are you telling me that the greatest enemy of workers' self-management is the party-and-state bureaucracy, when the greatest enemy is really the party-and-state bureaucracy?"[94]

- As in a new version of the old Jewish joke: "You are polite, so why do you act as if you were polite?"[95]

- This mystery of the symbolic order is exemplified by the enigmatic status of what we call "politeness": when, upon meeting an acquaintance, I say "Glad to see you! How are you today?" it is clear to both of us that, in a way, I "do not mean it seriously" (if my partner suspects that I am really interested, he may even be unpleasantly surprised, as though I were probing at something that is too intimate and of no concern to me—or, to paraphrase the old Freudian joke: "Why are you saying you're glad to see me, when you're *really* glad to see me!?").[96]

- This difference between the two appearances (the way things *really* appear to us versus the way they *appear* to appear to us) is linked to the structure of the Freudian joke about a Jew who complains to his friend, "Why are you telling me you are going to Lemberg when you are really going to Lemberg?": say, in the case of commodity fetishism, when I immediately perceive money as just a knot of social relations, not any kind of magic object, and I only treat it like a fetish in my practice, so that the site of fetishism is my actual social practice, I could effectively be reproached with: "Why are you saying that money is just a knot of social relations, when money really *is* just a knot of social relations?"[97]

- Consequently, one cannot but recall here the old Freudian joke of the Jew lying to his friend about the true destination of his voyage in the guise of truth itself: "Why did Clinton say that they should listen to the protesters, when they should effectively listen to the protesters?"[98]

- So, in the vein of Freud's well-known Jewish joke, "Why are you telling me that you are going to Lemberg, when you are effectively going to Lemberg?," the basic implicit reproach of the sucker-partner to the *femme fatale* could be formulated as "Why do you act as if you are just a cold manipulative bitch, when you really are just a cold manipulative bitch?"[99]

THE EFFECT OF THE REAL occurs in the joke about a patient who complains to his analyst that there is a big crocodile under his bed. The analyst explains to him that this is his paranoiac hallucination and gradually cures him, so the patient stops seeing him. A couple of months later, the analyst encounters on the street a friend of his ex-patient with the crocodile-idea and asks how him how the patient is doing; the friend replies: "Which one do you mean? The one who is now dead since he was eaten by a crocodile that was hiding under his bed?"[100]

THIS, HOWEVER, IS ONLY ONE SIDE of the phallus paradox; its reverse is indicated by a riddle/joke: "What is the lightest object on earth?—The phallus, because it is the only one that can be elevated by mere thought."[101]

VARIATION

• Erection depends entirely on me, on my mind (as the joke goes: "What is the lightest object in the world? The penis, because it is the only one that can be raised by a mere thought!"), yet it is simultaneously that over which I ultimately have no control (if I am not in the right mood, no amount of willpower will achieve it—that is why, for St. Augustine, the fact that erection escapes the control of my will is the divine punishment for man's arrogance and presumption, for his desire to become master of the universe.)[102]

"DID YOU HEAR THE ONE about a stupid worm trying to penetrate a puffy doughnut?"

"No."

"Neither did I."

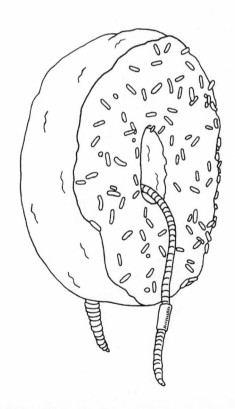

NOTES

Unless otherwise indicated, all of the jokes are from unpublished manuscripts.

1. *The Year of Dreaming Dangerously* (London: Verso, 2012), 39–40.
2. *Less Than Nothing* (London: Verso, 2012), 599.
3. Ibid., 538.
4. Ibid., 89.
5. Ibid., 325.
6. Ibid., 277.
7. Ibid., 494.
8. Ibid., 422.
9. Ibid., 696–697.
10. Ibid., 708–709.
11. Ibid., 745–746.
12. Ibid., 765–766.
13. Ibid., 788.
14. Ibid., 768.
15. *Living in the End Times* (London: Verso, 2010), 27.
16. Ibid., 401–402.
17. *The Monstrosity of Christ: Paradox or Dialectic?* (Cambridge, Mass.: MIT Press, 2009), 42.
18. Ibid., 286.
19. *Living in the End Times*, 299–300.
20. *Violence: Big Ideas/Small Books* (New York: Picador, 2008), 11.
21. *In Defense of Lost Causes* (London: Verso, 2008), 268.
22. Ibid., 306–307.
23. *The Monstrosity of Christ*, 270.

24. *The Sublime Object of Ideology* (London: Verso, 1989), 147.

25. *For They Know Not What They Do* (London: Verso, 1991), 173.

26. *In Defense of Lost Causes*, 318.

27. Ibid., 331.

28. *How to Read Lacan* (London: Granta Books, 2006), 69–70.

29. *The Parallax View* (Cambridge, Mass.: MIT Press, 2006), 64.

30. Ibid., 109–110.

31. Ibid., 178–179.

32. Ibid., 351.

33. *How to Read Lacan*, 43.

34. *The Parallax View*, 353.

35. Ibid., 401.

36. Ibid.

37. Ibid., 413.

38. *Interrogating the Real* (London: Continuum International Publishing Group, 2005), 13.

39. *Iraq: The Borrowed Kettle* (London: Verso, 2004), 4.

40. *Violence*, 44.

41. *Iraq*, 70.

42. Ibid., 132.

43. *The Puppet and the Dwarf: The Perverse Core of Christianity* (Cambridge, Mass.: MIT Press, 2003), 49.

44. Ibid., 101.

45. Ibid., 137–138.

46. Ibid., 182.

47. *Organs Without Bodies* (New York: Routledge, 2003), 58–59.

48. Ibid., 60.

49. Ibid., 61.

50. Ibid., 77–80.

51. Ibid., 158.

52. *Tarrying with the Negative* (Durham, N.C.: Duke University Press 1993), 74.

53. *Revolution at the Gates: Žižek on Lenin, the 1917 Writings* (London: Verso, 2002), 206.

54. *Welcome to the Desert of the Real* (London: Verso, 2002), 1.

55. Ibid., 3.

56. Ibid., 77.

57. Ibid., 92.

58. *On Belief* (London: Routledge, 2001).

59. *The Fright of Real Tears: Krzysztof Kieslowski Between Theory and Post-Theory* (London: British Film Institute, 2001), 29.

60. *Did Somebody Say Totalitarianism?* (London: Verso, 2001), 147.

61. Ibid., 190.

62. *The Fragile Absolute: Or, Why Is the Christian Legacy Worth Fighting For?* (London: Verso, 2000), 50.

63. Ibid., 50–51.

64. Ibid., 53–54.

65. *The Plague of Fantasies* (London: Verso, 1997), 25.

66. Ibid., 39.

67. Ibid., 46.

68. Ibid., 110.

69. Ibid., 172.

70. Ibid., 179.

71. Ibid., 188–189.

72. *The Indivisible Remainder: Essays on Schelling and Related Matters* (London: Verso, 1996), 198.

73. *Everything You Always Wanted to Know About Lacan … But Were Afraid to Ask Hitchcock* (London: Verso, 1993), 44.

74. *Tarrying with the Negative*, 244.

75. Ibid., 268.

76. *Enjoy Your Symptom!* (London: Routledge 1992), 10.

77. *The Sublime Object of Ideology*, 6–7.

78. Ibid., 29.

79. Ibid., 64.

80. *The Metastases of Enjoyment* (London: Verso, 1994), 143.

81. *The Sublime Object of Ideology*, 65.

82. Ibid., 66.

83. Ibid., 159.

84. Ibid., 160.

85. Ibid., 163.

86. Ibid., 175–176.

87. *Less Than Nothing*, 243.

88. Ibid., 1003.

89. Ibid., 530–531.

90. Ibid., 535.

91. Ibid., 538.

92. *For They Know Not What They Do*, 1.

93. *The Sublime Object of Ideology*, 197.

94. Ibid., 198.

95. *In Defense of Lost Causes*, 13.

96. *The Plague of Fantasies*, 110–111.

97. *The Universal Exception* (London: Continuum International Publishing Group, 2006), 316.

98. *Organs Without Bodies*, 145.

99. *The Art of the Ridiculous Sublime: On David Lynch's Lost Highway* (Seattle: University of Washington Press, 2000), 16.

100. *The Sublime Object of Ideology*, 212.

101. Ibid., 223.

102. *The Ticklish Subject* (London: Verso, 1999), 382–383.

*Comedy is a legitimacy crisis
followed by the sudden appearance
of a cornucopia*

There's a joke that appears twice in my *Book of Jokes* (a novel in which the story of a family is told entirely in jokes). I learned it from Žižek, who attributes it to Freud. "We all remember," says Žižek, at the start of a 2004 essay entitled "The Iraqi Borrowed Kettle," "the old joke about the borrowed kettle that Freud quotes in order to render the strange logic of dreams, namely the enumeration of mutually exclusive answers to a reproach (that I returned to a friend a broken kettle): (1) I never borrowed a kettle from you; (2) I returned it to you unbroken; (3) the kettle was already broken when I got it from you." Is this a joke, or is it a conundrum or a syndrome? It's a shape of situation, Žižek says. A structure.

Žižek seems to have a brain very much suited to the recognition of particular situational shapes. Thinking about something in the real world, he suddenly recognizes that it has the same basic structure as an absurd situation in a joke he's heard, often from a highly respectable source; Derrida, or Lacan, or Freud.

This technique gives us a refreshing sense of what we might call "the lightness of profundity." We see the charming playfulness of the great masters of philosophy, and perhaps begin to recognize philosophy itself, at its highest, lightest level, as something akin to laughter and joking; "the smile of the gods." Certain scenarios in the real world can be as absurd as jokes, self-evidently laughable, no matter how tragic they are.

History, Žižek likes to remind us—citing Marx, himself citing Hegel—plays first as tragedy, then as farce. And laughter at the farcical has a sublime aspect; it allows us to imagine the redundancy of one set of ideas, and the birth of a dizzying plethora of alternatives. Comedy is a legitimacy crisis followed by the sudden appearance of a cornucopia.

In my telling of the kettle story the situation becomes farcical by exaggeration. My father has been entrusted with the care of a pot plant while its owners, led by a small, prissy, semi-naked lawyer called Bernard Bernardson, go on holiday. My father forgets completely to water the plant, which consequently withers. He defends himself with the following list of self-justifications:

1. The plant had never been entrusted to him.

2. In fact, it was his plant.

3. The plant had been entrusted to him, but he had never promised to return it in good condition.

4. He had sworn to the gods to ruin the plant, and was simply fulfilling his promise.

5. There was nothing whatsoever wrong with the plant.

6. He wished he'd never borrowed the plant, it was withered from the moment he set eyes on it.

7. This species of plant is withered from birth or, rather, is wither-proof.

8. The plant withered despite his best efforts. It was beset by a plague of flies.

9. Withering is only bad because we are conditioned to think of it as such.

10. In fact, healthy green sprouting is the most painful thing for a plant to endure.

11. Healthy green sprouting is an abomination.

12. Withering—warmly welcomed by sensible plants—is "the new" healthy green sprouting.

13. Therefore withering is good, because healthy green sprouting is good.

14. On the contrary, healthy green sprouting is abominable, and therefore withering is abominable.

15. Nothing as bad as withering could have happened to the plant under my watch. Therefore it has not withered.

16. Healthy plants have gone out of fashion during your absence.

17. This is not the same plant you left me.

18. This is, nevertheless and despite appearances, a healthy plant.

19. Look, there, behind you! A kitten!

20. The plant has committed suicide.

My father is a monstrous character in the book, and yet we cannot help liking him. This "kettle list" of excuses has a low motivation—the covering-up of an act of neglect—but its attenuation, inventiveness, ingenuity, and illogicality begin to amuse and refresh us, like a Cubist painting of the situation that may not add up to anything like "the truth," but begins to dazzle us with a sense of sheer possibility, or like a clever child's answers to a psychologist's Uses of Objects test. We begin to see, alongside the merely legitimate, or the merely correct, the possibility of a cornucopia.

Because we live in a society that massively prefers control to creativity, telling the truth has been vastly overrated. "Every lie creates the parallel world in which it is true." This is the aphorism that guides my *Book of Scotlands*, a series of scenarios imagining, deliriously, alternative futures for my northern British motherland. Lies can be generative, they can help us brainstorm our way out of stale, dead-end ways of thinking. Jokes have the same capacity; by overturning the logic of clichés based on what are undoubtedly true and correct ways of understanding the world, jokes give us a tingling and vertiginous sense of alternative possibilities. Political pundits have a term called the Overton Window. It describes the sort of centrist agenda a politician may embrace without any danger of being called a crank or an extremist, and the ways he may shift that window of acceptability a few degrees to the left or right. The dogged pursuit of consensus and compromise based, precisely, on a lack of any fresh or original thinking may be crucial for a career politician, but it spells death to anyone who's mentally alive. The "mentally alive"—and in this category good writers are found—will surely prefer the logic of jokes, which by their very nature stray outside the Overton Window, transgress against common sense and accepted morality, and breach taboos.

Let's say that the world divides into those who want to be right, and those who want to be interesting. The Right usually have an eye on instrumental power over man and over nature. Their rightness is a means to that power. The Interesting wish to charm, beguile, teach, astound, influence, outrage, confuse. What power they possess is predicated on a renunciation of actual, instrumental power.

I would not want the captain of my jet to be interesting; I would prefer him to be right. But I would like the in-flight movie to be as interesting as possible. In contrast to events in the cockpit, whatever happens in the movie, the plane will not crash. In my own (real) family, my brother, an academic, is the Right one and I am the Interesting one. I first heard of Žižek through my brother, who described him to me as "crazy, a hothead." Interesting, perhaps, but untrustworthy. Not a solid chap, but an interestingly unreliable narrator of history, a wearer of clown motley, a Shakespearean Fool. My brother must have known that, based on this sketch, I would become a fan.

Žižek's unreliability is underlined by the fact that he re-tells the same jokes in different forms. As if enacting in his texts a kind of synthetic version of the oral folk culture from which jokes originate, he rings the same joke through a series of changes, reporting different origins, outcomes and moral applications each time.

Žižek risks giving the appearance of a slightly absent-minded old uncle at a wedding, who doesn't remember that he told us the same joke at another family gathering recently, or perhaps does remember but finds the joke so funny and so effective that he can't help tell it again, but with its attributions, pedigree, wording, length and degree of obscenity tailored (suspiciously, we might say) to the new context.

And so the fiancée joke ("my fiancée is never late for an appointment, because the moment she is late, she is no longer my fiancée") makes an appearance in several of his books, attributed variously to Lacan and to an "old proverb," and interpreted, like the broken kettle, in an incompatibly wide variety of different applications. According to Žižek, and according to situation, the fiancée joke implies:

1. That "the People always support the Party because any member of the People who opposes Party rule automatically excludes himself from the People."

2. That "if you love God, you can do whatever you like, because when you do something evil, this is in itself a proof that you do not really love God."

3. That "a Truth is never enforced, because the moment the fidelity to Truth functions as an excessive enforcement, we are no longer dealing with a Truth, with fidelity to a Truth-Event."

4. That "I never make a mistake in applying a rule, since what I do defines the very rule."

5. And that, most gnomically of all, "here also, the fiancée is reduced to her symbolic function of fiancée." In the terms of another favorite Žižek joke, why do you claim to be a fiancée when you are actually a fiancée?

Allowing Žižek to boil complex situations down until they can be identified with jokes has benefits for the reader. It is as if the joke has become for Žižek what algebra is for his old ally and rival Badiou: the most concise way Žižek knows to sum up a universal situational shape. Unlike algebra, however, the joke brings with it, simply by virtue of being a joke, the liberating implication that the situation described is no longer inherently legitimate or inevitable. Identifying it as something laughable gives us the impression that it is also something that can be left behind. Laughter is, in this sense, revolutionary.

Not content to use Žižek's Freud Kettle joke just once in my *Book of Jokes*, I revisit in the form of a joke about a doll. Luisa is complaining that her father has borrowed a doll called Hanna and returned it broken:

> "That's the worst thing," said Luisa. "He told me he'd never borrowed Hanna in the first place, and that when he'd given her back to me Hanna hadn't been broken. Then he added that Hanna had already been broken when he'd first borrowed her, and that a broken doll is in fact more charming than an unbroken one, and that therefore it was a real shame Hanna wasn't in fact broken …"

> "But she was broken!"

> "Yes, she was broken all right. Then he told me that, in a sense, every broken doll is whole and every unbroken doll is in fragments."

> "He's a nutter!"

> "He's a nutter, all right. He followed that with the information that Hanna both was and was not broken, depending on how you looked at it. Then he said that, although the doll was mine, her brokenness was his, and

that he had broken Hanna for her own good. Then Dad
started to cry and said that nothing could replace my
broken Hanna, so 'Here's nothing!' And he made as if to
hand me nothing."

"Honestly! The fuckface!"

"He wasn't finished, either. He told me—quite seriously—
that what's important now is not the unbroken doll, but how
she has broken our hearts, therefore making us whole and
joining us together. 'We have all been broken by this non-
doll Hanna,' he said, 'who has therefore healed us.' I was
weeping too by this point. He's a clever old bastard, Dad."

"He is, too."

I'm not entirely joking when I say that Žižek is my father.

BIBLIOGRAPHY

2012   *The Year of Dreaming Dangerously*. London: Verso

2012   *Less Than Nothing: Hegel and the Shadow of Dialectical Materialism*. London: Verso

2010   *Living in the End Times*. London: Verso.

2009   *Philosophy in the Present*. Cambridge: Polity (with Alain Badiou).

2009   *Mythology, Madness and Laughter: Subjectivity in German Idealism*. London/New York: Continuum International Publishing Group (with Markus Gabriel).

2009   *First As Tragedy, Then As Farce*. London: Verso.

2009   *In Search of Wagner (Radical Thinkers)*. London: Verso (selected texts of Theodor W. Adorno with introduction by Žižek).

2009   *The Monstrosity of Christ: Paradox or Dialectic?* Cambridge, Mass.: MIT Press (with John Milbank).

2008   *Violence: Big Ideas/Small Books*. New York: Picador.

2008   *In Defense of Lost Causes*. London: Verso.

2006   *How to Read Lacan*. London: Granta Books.

2006   *The Parallax View*. Cambridge, Mass.: MIT Press.

2006   *The Universal Exception*. London/New York: Continuum International Publishing Group.

2005   *Interrogating the Real*. London/New York: Continuum
        International Publishing Group.

2004   *Iraq: The Borrowed Kettle*. London: Verso.

2003   *The Puppet and the Dwarf: The Perverse Core of Christianity*.
        Cambridge, Mass.: MIT Press.

2003   *Organs Without Bodies*. London: Routledge.

2002   *Revolution at the Gates: Žižek on Lenin, the 1917 Writings*.
        London: Verso.

2002   *Welcome to the Desert of the Real*. London: Verso.

2001   *On Belief*. London: Routledge.

2001   *Opera's Second Death*. New York: Routledge.

2001   *The Fright of Real Tears: Krzysztof Kieślowski Between Theory and
        Post-Theory*. London: British Film Institute (BFI).

2001   *Did Somebody Say Totalitarianism?* London: Verso.

2000   *The Fragile Absolute: Or, Why is the Christian Legacy Worth
        Fighting For?* London: Verso.

2000   *The Art of the Ridiculous Sublime: On David Lynch's Lost
        Highway*. Seattle: University of Washington Press.

2000   *Contingency, Hegemony, Universality* (with Judith Butler and
        Ernesto Laclau). London: Verso.

1999   *The Ticklish Subject*. London: Verso.

1997   *The Plague of Fantasies*. London: Verso.

1996   *The Indivisible Remainder: Essays on Schelling and Related
        Matters*. London: Verso.

1994   *The Metastases of Enjoyment*. London: Verso.

1993   *Everything You Always Wanted to Know About Lacan ... But Were Afraid to Ask Hitchcock*. London: Verso.

1993   *Tarrying with the Negative*. Durham, N.C.: Duke University Press.

1992   *Enjoy Your Symptom!* New York: Routledge.

1991   *Looking Awry*. Cambridge, Mass.: MIT Press.

1991   *For They Know Not What They Do*. London: Verso.

1989   *The Sublime Object of Ideology*. London: Verso.

ABOUT THE CONTRIBUTORS

Slavoj Žižek is a philosopher and cultural critic. He has published over thirty books, including *Looking Awry*, *The Puppet and the Dwarf*, and *The Parallax View* (these three published by the MIT Press).

Audun Mortensen, born in 1985, is the author of two poetry books, a novel, and a coffee table book version of *The Collected Jokes of Slavoj Žižek* (2011) in a limited edition of 1. He lives in Berlin.

Momus, born Nick Currie in Scotland in 1960, is the author of more than twenty albums of songs and three books. His first novel, published in 2008, was *The Book of Jokes*, an account of an extremely dysfunctional family destined to live out their lives as characters locked in a series of dirty and cruel jokes. His latest album is *Bibliotek* (2012), cast in a genre he calls "pastoral horror." Momus lives in Osaka, Japan.

Žižek's Jokes
(Did you hear the one about Hegel and negation?)
SLAVOJ ŽIŽEK

Unlike any other book by Slavoj Žižek, this compact arrangement of jokes—some "nicely vulgar" (his term) and some not so nicely vulgar—culled from his writings provides an index to certain philosophical, political, and sexual themes that preoccupy him. *Žižek's Jokes* contains the set-ups and punch lines—as well as the offenses and insults—that Žižek is famous for, all in about 150 pages.

For Žižek, jokes are amusing stories that offer a shortcut to philosophical insight. He illustrates the logic of the Hegelian triad, for example, with three variations of the "Not tonight, dear, I have a headache" classic: first the wife claims a migraine; then the husband does; then the wife exclaims, "Darling, I have a terrible migraine, so let's have some sex to refresh me!" A punch line about a beer bottle provides a Lacanian lesson about one signifier. And a "truly obscene" version of the famous "aristocrats" joke has the family offering a short course in Hegelian thought rather than a display of unspeakables.

Žižek's Jokes contains every joke cited, paraphrased, or narrated in Žižek's work in English (including some in unpublished manuscripts), including different versions of the same joke that make different points in different contexts. The larger point being that comedy is central to Žižek's seriousness.

SLAVOJ ŽIŽEK is a philosopher and cultural critic. He is the author of more than thirty books, including *Looking Awry: An Introduction to Jacques Lacan through Popular Culture*, *The Puppet and the Dwarf: The Perverse Core of Christianity*, *The Parallax View*, and (with John Milbank) *The Monstrosity of Christ: Paradox or Dialectic?*, these four published by the MIT Press.

Endleaf photographs by Hendrik Speck at European Graduate School. 2008.
Copyright: European Graduate School